NAPOLEON'S
ELITE CAVALRY

NAPOLEON'S ELITE CAVALRY

Cavalry of the Imperial Guard, 1804–1815

Paintings by Lucien Rousselot
Text by Edward Ryan

GREENHILL BOOKS, LONDON
STACKPOLE BOOKS, PENNSYLVANIA

FRONTISPIECE: PLATE 1

The Emperor Napoleon

Rousselot painted Napoleon on numerous occasions, depicting him in a variety of situations and at different stages of his career. Here he shows us Napoleon at the apogee of the Empire, carrying out a review in the Place de l'Arc de Triomphe du Carrousel and passing before the *Grenadiers à cheval* of the Imperial Guard, a stern-looking marshal following close behind. He is wearing the uniform of a colonel of the *Chasseurs à cheval* of the Guard, his almost invariable choice when he was on campaign and the uniform in which he was interred in Saint Helena. His decorations are the Star of the *Légion d'Honneur* and the *Couronne de Fer*. The embroidered *Grand-Aigle* of the Legion is sewn to his jacket, its ribbon passing down to his hip.

Less frequently, Napoleon chose the uniform of a colonel of the *Chasseurs à pied* of the Guard, in which he appeared at Tilsit, Eckmühl, Wagram and Waterloo. In 1814, and after his return from Elba, he often wore the uniform of the National Guard, perhaps to demonstrate solidarity with his young National Guard soldiers.

During his career, Napoleon owned more than a hundred horses of various breeds. (At Saint Helena, he said that eighteen of them had been killed under him on the battlefield.) While whites and light greys were his favourites, many were bays and chestnuts. The stuffed remains of *Le Vizir*, an Arab horse said to have accompanied Napoleon to Saint Helena, may be seen in the *Musée de l'Armée*.

While not a graceful rider, in his prime the Emperor was a fearless and indefatigable horseman. Once he rode from Valladolid to Burgos, a distance of some 57 miles, in three and a half hours, leaving his escort trailing behind.

Napoleon's Elite Cavalry first published 1999
by Greenhill Books, Lionel Leventhal Limited, Park House, 1 Russell Gardens, London NW11 9NN
and
Stackpole Books, 5067 Ritter Road, Mechanicsburg, PA 17055, USA

British Library Cataloguing in Publication Data
Rousselot, Lucien
Napoleon's elite cavalry: cavalry of the Imperial Guard, 1804–1815
1. France. Armee. Garde imperiale – Cavalry – Pictorial works
2. Napoleonic Wars, 1800–1815 – Campaigns – Pictorial works
I. Title   II. Ryan, Edward
940.2'7

ISBN 1-85367-371-4

Library of Congress Cataloging-in-Publication Data available

Printed and bound in Singapore

CONTENTS

Garde Impériale – Chevau-légers Polonais. 1807–1814

Appendices

Bibliography

Lucien Rousselot
(courtesy of *La Sabretache*)

PREFACE

Lucien Rousselot
1900–92
Peintre de l'Armée
Chevalier de la Légion d'Honneur
Officier des Arts et des Lettres
Chevalier des Palmes Academiques
Membre de La Sabretache

Regarded by the most knowledgeable of his contemporaries as the creator of the science of uniformology, Lucien Rousselot is also seen as the last of the line of renowned French military painters, beginning with Meissonier, and continuing with de Neuville and Detaille. But not for Rousselot were the grand, sweeping battle scenes that won so much acclaim for his predecessors, although his smaller-scale paintings of eighteenth- and nineteenth-century French troops on campaign and in combat were sought after by public institutions and private collectors. His art is of a more intimate character, which combines his exceptional technical skills as an artist and a relentless determination to achieve absolute authenticity.

For almost eighty years, Rousselot applied those qualities to produce what is generally accepted as one of the most thoroughly documented and accurately depicted records of French military uniforms, arms and equipment as they evolved from the early eighteenth century to the middle of the twentieth century.

As Rousselot began to make a name for himself among military historians and artists, in 1919 joining the prestigious society of 'collectors of figurines and friends of military history', *La Sabretache*, he became increasingly aware that, occasionally, some of his greatly admired predecessors had relied upon questionable sources for their documentation. These included the ageing memories of old soldiers.

Consequently, in 1925 Rousselot began a systematic search of hundreds of boxes of records in the archives of the army. There, among other things, he found samples of uniform cloth that had never been exposed to the fading effect of sunlight, reports of inspectors general, and even examples of uniforms and equipment.

Rousselot described his best sources as contemporary iconography, contemporary paintings, miniatures, naïve portraits (often of absolute fidelity, he said), archives, reports and correspondence.

It was not long before he became accepted by French military historians and uniformologists as a leading expert on the design of French uniforms, arms and equipment. Increasingly, his opinions on these subjects were sought by individuals and institutions alike. In due course, he was elected a member of the Scientific Council of the *Musée de l'Armée*.

All of this recognition did nothing, however, to alter his modest and generous attitude toward all who sought his assistance. Invariably he responded to requests for information from colleagues, friends and even first-time visitors to his *atelier*. His personal qualities, which were often remarked upon, were his simplicity, patience and good humour, tempered at times by a caustic wit.

My own family had the privilege – I may say, the honour – of coming to know Lucien and Renée Rousselot, and to benefit from their generous hospitality during the several years we spent in Paris in the 1960s. It was typical of the artist that, when we finally left for home, he presented our twelve-year-old daughter with a beautiful paper figure of Napoleon, inscribed, '*A notre petite Amie, Cordelia Ryan.*' For the next twenty years, my Christmas greetings from Rousselot took the form of hand-painted figures of Napoleonic soldiers.

Rousselot's *chef d'oeuvre*, for which he is most widely known, is his series of 106 *planches* (plates) on the uniforms, arms and equipment of the French Army: *L'Armée Française – ses Uniformes – son Armement – son Equipment*. Begun in 1943, the *planches*, with their accompanying texts rich in detail, were published periodically in groups of two or three. They covered the evolution of the French Army's uniforms and equipage from 1720 to 1870, the last of them being published in 1971. The series is unique for the quality of its execution and for its accuracy. The original edition having long since been exhausted, in recent years the series has been reprinted.

Readers of this volume, who possess the *planches* of Rousselot's series that pertain to the four Guard cavalry regiments, will detect a few discrepancies between the two works. I believe that the explanation for those contradictions is simple: in the years after he had completed these paintings (the 1950s), his continuing research revealed new information that he believed was more accurate. In a letter he wrote to me in January 1989, after I had told him of my hope to see the ninety-one paintings published, he pointed out errors in two of the paintings. One related to the kettledrummer of the Dragoons (Plate 56), and the other to the trumpeters of the *Chevau-légers Polonais* (Plate 76). His comments concerning each painting will be found in the text accompanying those plates.

The subjects of Rousselot's paintings are rendered with remarkable artistic skill, being given an additional sense of immediacy and reality by his exceptional ability to portray convincingly the men who wore those brilliant uniforms, wielded those glittering arms and rode those brave horses, 'printing their proud hoofs i' the receiving earth' of the battlefields of the Empire. The calm, resolute countenances of these men, with their natural, self-assured and graceful postures, tell us that they are veterans, and masters of their trade. One would have been proud to have been among their number.

From the time that he became a member of *La Sabretache* until almost the end of his life, Rousselot was one of its most generous contributors, providing it with a great many uniform plates and descriptive texts. From 1921 to 1945, his work frequently appeared in the pages of *Passepoil* as well.

Rousselot accumulated a relatively modest collection of military artefacts, which included some unique examples of First Empire uniforms and equipment. As gifted a sculptor and artisan as he was a painter, he put those talents to use by creating 40cm scale models of horses and their riders. The miniature barracks he created for his cuirassiers and chasseurs – complete with exquisitely made arms, saddles and harness – was a source of utter fascination for his visitors. Madame Rousselot assumed part of the responsibility for dressing these small-scale troopers by, for example, painstakingly sewing on the dozens of tiny buttons on a chasseur's pelisse.

Between 1964 and 1970, Rousselot published four series of small folders under the title, *Soldats d'Autrefois* (Soldiers of Bygone Days), each of which contained six plates. The subjects of the four series were *Carabiniers*, *Hussards*, *Gardes d'honneur* and *Mameluks* of the Napoleonic Army. To celebrate the Bicentenary of the Emperor's birth in 1969, he issued *Napoléon*, a portfolio of twelve colour plates, showing the Emperor at various moments of his career.

To identify completely the many other examples of Rousselot's 'art in the service of history' would be well nigh impossible, since his contributions were so numerous and wide-ranging. He designed lead soldiers for the famous *Petits soldats de France* of Madame Fernande Metayer, and provided the designs for several series of 30 mm 'flats' for the equally well-known Parisian firm, Mignot.

In 1953, a series of forty-two Rousselot paintings, *Les cavaliers de Bonaparte*, illustrating the uniforms of twenty-one regiments of dragoons, was published by Roulleau in a limited edition of forty copies. Marcel Dupont's *Cavaliers d'Epopée*, published in 1985, was richly illustrated by Rousselot. In 1976, he painted 160 illustrations for R. Petitmermet's *Schweizer Uniformen – Uniformes suisses 1700–1850*.

The *Musée de l'Armée* possesses two series of Rousselot's watercolours depicting the French Army of Egypt, 1798–1800, and the French Army in Algeria.

The paintings in this volume were produced by Rousselot on commission from Anne Brown, being delivered to her in 1957. It seems probable that he had been working on them for some time, perhaps several years previously. Four of them were used as illustrations in Mrs Brown's book, *The Anatomy of Glory* (her translation of Henry Lachouque's *Napoléon et la Garde Impériale*), and a few have been reproduced, with the permission of the Brown Collection, for sale as individual prints. Otherwise, most of these paintings are being published for the first time.

I first became aware of the paintings when visiting the Brown Collection in the late 1980s. At the time, I was struck by the fact that this very rich pictorial material, produced by arguably France's greatest military artist, was almost totally unknown – and unavailable – to the very large number of admirers of his work around the world. I concluded that some way ought to be found to bring these paintings to the public. In fact, I regard it as an obligation to *Maître* Rousselot to perform this service, even though, regrettably, he is no longer here to appreciate it, in return for the many kindnesses that he

and Madame Rousselot had rendered to my family those many years ago.

Since then, the curator of the Brown Collection, Peter Harrington, and I have searched for a means of introducing these beautiful paintings to an audience that we believe will find in them a major addition to the already very rich heritage of Lucien Rousselot. Now, thanks to the vision and enthusiasm of Lionel Leventhal, publisher of Greenhill Books, we are able to realise that aspiration. We are greatly in his debt.

In a very real sense, this volume is also a tribute to the remarkable founder of one of the most extensive private collections of historical military information in the world, Anne S.K. Brown. The collection that bears her name is a valuable source of reference for historians, uniformologists, art collectors, experts and publishers world-wide. These paintings are but a small sample of the riches to be found in The Anne S.K. Brown Military Collection, which is housed in the John Hay Library of Brown University, in Providence, Rhode Island.

Gathered over a period of some forty years, the collection was presented by Mrs Brown to Brown University in 1981. Ever since, it has continued to grow in size and scope. At present, it comprises over 12,000 books, 18,000 albums, sketchbooks, scrapbooks and portfolios (which themselves contain thousands of prints and drawings), over 13,000 individual works of art, and a spectacular display of more than 5000 model soldiers, as well as an exceptional collection of uncut sheets of paper soldiers, representing fighting men and their units from the days of ancient Egypt to the twentieth century.

I owe a special word of thanks to Peter Harrington for his continued encouragement and assistance in pursuit of this goal, and his unstinting support in my research at the Brown Collection. I am also grateful to Monsieur Albert Rigondaud ('RIGO') for his kind amplification of the circumstances surrounding the creation of these paintings. I am no less indebted to Monsieur Guy Démoulin for his advice in respect of French uniform terminology.

I have relied very heavily on Rousselot's own texts for information regarding the uniforms illustrated. Anne Brown's superb translation of Henry Lachouque's *Napoléon et la Garde Impériale* has been of enormous help to me, as has been the indispensable *Swords Around a Throne*, by Colonel John Elting. As for other sources, the Bibliography will speak for itself.

Sometime after writing this Preface, I came across a letter from Rousselot dated 31 January 1989. The preceding December I had written to tell him of my coming across these paintings in the stacks of the Anne S. K. Brown Collection, and of my hope to see them published. Writing in French he replied:

'I would very much like to see the watercolours, which I made about 1950 and which are now part of the documentation brought together by Mrs Brown, published.'

I greatly regret that the fulfillment of that aspiration, expressed ten years ago, has come too late for my friend to be able to share my gratification at seeing its realisation.

Edward Ryan, 1999

INTRODUCTION

The subjects for this suite of Rousselot's paintings are the most prestigious of Napoleon's cavalry regiments, the elite of the Imperial Guard cavalry: the *Chasseurs à cheval*, the *Grenadiers à cheval*, the *Dragons de l'Impératrice* and the *Chevau-légers Polonais*. The artist has depicted them on parade, in quieter moments on duty and during their off-duty hours, on campaign and in combat.

This brief review of the creation of each of these regiments, their organisational evolution during the life of the Empire, and the role that they played in Napoleon's principal campaigns is intended to provide readers with a background for the paintings and their accompanying texts. It is my hope that an understanding of what it meant to be part of that extraordinary military phalanx, the Imperial Guard, may further enhance a reader's appreciation of these exceptionally fine, highly evocative works of art.

Although the paintings do not depict men of other Guard cavalry regiments and formations that fought alongside the four elite regiments, inevitably the names and roles of some of them will occur in the text, as the units were integrated in terms of organisation and operations. The other cavalry units of the Guard, which are outside the framework of this book, are identified in Appendix II.

The Consular Guard of the French Republic, which was transformed by Napoleon into his Imperial Guard in 1804, had its origins in two bodies. These had been formed in Paris, in the wake of the Revolution, to serve as guards for the new legislature and for the members of the Directory.

The *Garde du Corps legislatif* had evolved through a number of earlier incarnations: from the Guards of the Assembly, to the National Gendarmes, to the Grenadier-Gendarmes, to the Grenadiers of the National Representatives, and finally to the Grenadiers of the Legislature, or the *Garde du Corps legislatif*. The 1200 men of this body, most of them seasoned campaigners drawn from the ranks of the regular army, were divided into seven companies.

In 1796, the *Garde du Directoire executif* was formed to serve as an escort for the Directors on public occasions. (In a curious throw-back to the *Ancien Régime*, it was referred to in a decree of 1798 as the *Maison de la Directoire*.) This corps included two companies of Foot Grenadiers, two of Horse Grenadiers and a twenty-five-piece band formed by musicians from the Paris Conservatory of Music.

Two other groups included in the formation of the Consular Guard were 180 *Guides à cheval* and 125 *Guides à pied*, selected by Bonaparte from the *Corps des Guides d'Etat-major de l'Armée de l'Orient*. That unit, in turn, had its origins in the squadron of *Guides* originally created by Kellermann, which Bonaparte had taken over in Italy in 1796, as his own personal guard in his capacity as Commander-in-Chief of the Army of Italy.

When Bonaparte left Egypt for France on 23 August 1799, the *Guides* travelled with him, staging in the Midi while he proceeded to Paris. Following the success of the coup of 18/19 *Brumaire* (9/10 November 1799), Bonaparte summoned them to Paris, and by 17 December they were lodged in the *Caserne de Babylone*.

On the evening of 19 *Brumaire*, the troops of the *Garde du Corps legislatif* and the *Garde du Directoire executif* were amalgamated to become the *Garde des Consuls*. This was formalised in a decree of 28 November 1799. The initial strength of the unit was some 1200 men. On 2 December, Joachim Murat, already a lieutenant-general, was made Commander-in-Chief and Inspector General of the *Garde des Consuls*. By May of the following year, however, he had moved on to a higher position, as Commander of Cavalry of the *Armée de reserve*, which had been launched into another campaign in Italy. His replacement as commander of the Consular Guard was Jean Lannes.

On 3 January 1800, a decree established the structure of the new Guard. Its prescribed strength was 2089 men, divided among a general staff, two battalions of grenadiers, a battalion of chasseurs, three squadrons of light cavalry (actually, the Horse Grenadiers of the *Garde du Directoire executif*), a squadron of *chasseurs à cheval*, a company of light artillery (including a detachment of horse artillery) and fifty musicians distributed between the infantry and cavalry. (The 'light cavalry' designation soon gave way to the more appropriate *grenadiers à cheval*.) As additional units – more cavalry squadrons, an artillery train, sailors, *vélites* – were added to the Consular Guard, by September 1800, its strength had grown to 3700 men.

As commander of the Consular Guard, Lannes' enthusiasm for showy and very expensive uniforms for his troops soon landed him in serious trouble with the First Consul. Having learned in November 1801 that Lannes had been wildly overspending the Guard's budget on sprucing up the guardsmen, Bonaparte replaced him with Jean Bessières, who had been commander of the Guard cavalry. A much chastened Lannes was dispatched on a diplomatic mission to Portugal.

Upon the formation of the Consular Guard, Bonaparte established the requirements for its men. Candidates had to be less than twenty-five years of age, and be between 5 ft 6 in and 6 ft tall. They had to have a minimum of ten years' service and have fought in at least three campaigns, or have the equivalent in wounds received in action; they had to be able to read and write; and they had to have displayed patriotism, bravery, discipline and exemplary conduct. With few variations, these requirements remained in effect throughout the duration of the Empire, although in its waning days, when manpower shortages made it difficult to bring depleted regiments up to strength, some of them were dropped.

By an order of the day on 10 May 1804, what had been

a purely governmental guard became the Imperial Guard, an elite corps at the disposition of the Emperor and an army within an army. Its status was formally established by a decree of 29 July 1804, which fixed its composition. By virtue of the order of 10 May, the *Chasseurs à cheval* and the *Grenadiers à cheval* became the first cavalry regiments of the *Garde Impériale*. Having distinguished himself as commander of the Consular Guard, Bessières inherited command of the new Guard.

It would be another two years before the third of the elite Guard cavalry regiments, the *Dragons de l'Impératrice*, would be established and, after that, almost another year before the fourth, the *Chevau-légers Polonais*, came into being.

The composition of the regiments evolved to meet the demands of different military situations and, to a degree, because of combat attrition. While the regiments frequently operated as integral elements of the Guard, and in close co-operation with one another, there were many instances when some of their squadrons were detached for duty in distant parts of the Empire. In the final years, on occasion Young Guard squadrons were brigaded separately from their Old Guard comrades within the army as a whole.

As has been noted, the *Chasseurs à cheval* were formed as a single squadron of the Consular Guard on 3 January 1800. In its initial strength of four officers and 113 men, it was under the command of Captain Eugène de Beauharnais. On 5 March, de Beauharnais was promoted to *chef d'escadron*, and by 8 September, the squadron consisted of two companies, totalling 234 men. In May 1801, the squadron was attached to the Horse Grenadiers. Although the Chasseurs had originally been formed as an escort for Bonaparte, at Marengo they fought alongside their Grenadier comrades as well.

On 14 November 1801, the Chasseurs were constituted as an independent regiment, with *Chef d'escadron* de Beauharnais still in command, and on 1 October 1802, it became a fully formed regiment of four squadrons, with fifty-six officers and 959 men. At the same time, de Beauharnais became a *chef de brigade*. By March 1805, he was a *général de brigade*, and two months later, he became Viceroy of Italy. He retained nominal command of the regiment, however, although actual command was exercised by Major Morland, as *Colonel-Commandant en second*.

Although Rousselot did not devote any of the paintings in this series to the Mameluks, when the composition of the Guard was established on 29 July 1804, administration of the company of Mameluks (at that time consisting of 109 men) became the responsibility of the Chasseurs. From then on, the Mameluks accompanied the Chasseurs across Europe, from Moravia to Spain to Russia and back, until the saga ended on 18 June 1815 at Waterloo. After the Mameluks had distinguished themselves at Austerlitz, Napoleon awarded them an eagle, with a guidon-shaped tricolour standard.

The Chasseurs were very conscious of the special place they occupied in Napoleon's affections, as his *enfants chéris* (pet children), and occasionally permitted themselves liberties that no other Guardsmen would have thought of taking. But the Emperor's tolerance was not limitless and occasionally arrogant behaviour on their part had a price. None could have exceeded their devotion to Napoleon, however, and he knew that when he committed them at a critical stage in a battle, their reckless courage and unsurpassed fighting qualities would, more often than not, prove decisive.

The *Grenadiers à cheval* were the most carefully selected, most envied and most feared of all French cavalry regiments. They were the supreme reserve, guarded jealously by Napoleon as his ultimate means of intimidation for overcoming a perilous situation. At one point, 300 of the 2000 men of the regiment held the *Legion d'Honneur*; every officer was a member of the Legion. Their habitual demeanour was one of cold aloofness, and they rarely smiled. Even when on foot, they maintained an air of gravity and personal dignity. They had the honour of being members of the *Grenadiers à cheval*, and that was sufficient. There were fewer *coquetteries* in their dress than in that of the other Guard cavalry regiments. They accepted with no embarrassment their nicknames of 'the gods' or 'gros talons' (big heels). The impressive image created by their towering bearskins and sombre, dark uniforms was literally heightened by the powerful black horses they rode.

When it was formed, in 1796, the cadre for the regiment was drawn from the Third Regiment of Dragoons. In February 1797, it became the *Grenadiers à cheval* and its men were given their bearskin caps. When the *Garde des Consuls* was formed in November 1799, the regiment's initial strength was two squadrons, later increased to three, and finally to four on 14 November 1801. It would remain at that strength until the formation of the Imperial Guard.

As a regiment of the Imperial Guard, its composition was of four squadrons, each of two companies: a total of 1018 men. Michel Ordener, who had commanded the Horse Guards under the Consulate, retained its command. Each company was led by a captain, assisted by two *lieutenants en premier*, two *lieutenants en second* and two *sous-lieutenants*. The regimental staff included a trumpet-major, two *brigadier-trompettes* and a *timbalier*. Each company had three *trompettes*. In September 1805, two squadrons of *vélites* were added. On campaign, the *Grenadiers à cheval* were divided into two regiments, each commanded by a major, under the overall command of the Grenadiers' colonel.

The Grenadiers were mounted on black Normandy horses with black manes and tails. They stood 14½–15 hands high, and would have been four or five years old when purchased.

Since the French Army included thirty dragoon regiments when the Imperial Guard was created by Napoleon in 1804, it may be surprising that two years passed before he decided to add a regiment of dragoons to the Guard cavalry. There were probably several reasons for Napoleon's decision. It seems clear that he wished to honour those thirty Line dragoon regiments, which had distinguished themselves so effectively in preceding campaigns. At the same time, he was following a military fashion of the time, given the existence of Prussian and British guard dragoon regiments (although the latter were 'guard' in title only). Certainly it had not escaped Napoleon's attention that Queen Louise of Prussia, colonel of the 5th Regiment of Dragoons – *Regiment der Königin* – had been appearing ostentatiously in uniform at the head of its squadrons on parade.

The date of the decree that reorganised the Imperial Guard, 15 April 1806, served as the birth date of the

Dragoons. The regiment would be organised in the same manner as the Chasseurs and the Grenadiers. Each of the dragoon Line regiments was required to furnish twelve men having at least ten years' service. The NCOs and *brigadiers* were to come from the Guard Chasseurs and Grenadiers. The Emperor himself would select the officers: two-thirds from the Chasseurs and Grenadiers, the remainder from the Line dragoons. Only two squadrons would be formed in the first year; in the following year, a new levy of ten men per Line regiment would make up the additional two squadrons. The definitive organisation of the regiment would be effective from 1 July, whereas the staff and the squadron of *vélites* were to be formed immediately.

To command the new regiment, Napoleon chose a cousin on his mother's side, Colonel Jean-Toussant Arrighi de Casanova, a brilliant cavalry officer who had made a name for himself in Egypt, Syria and Germany, and who had been wounded four times. (For that matter, Ordener had achieved some fame by receiving seven sabre wounds, three bullet wounds and a wound from a cannon ball in a single battle while in the Army of Helvetia.) As the cadre for his regiment, Arrighi had two majors (both with the rank of colonel), eight *chefs d'escadron*, a dozen captains and fifty lieutenants.

When the first two squadrons had been formed, they were presented to the Empress Josephine at a parade in the garden of the Tuileries. Charmed by the elegance of the new corps, the Empress decided – no doubt with some encouragement – to act as the regiment's godmother. The public was quick to dub it *les Dragons de l'Impératrice*, although this title was never given any official recognition.

Frédéric Masson observed that the formation of the Dragoons of the Guard marked the apogee of the army, but at the same time, led to its deterioration, because to create the regiment, the best men and veterans were taken from the Line dragoon regiments.

The creation of the *Chevau-légers Polonais*, somewhat less than a year later, was the result of an entirely different set of circumstances. The idea of Poles serving in, or under the command of, the French Army was nothing new, since Polish Legions, paid by France, had served in Italy under the Consulate and at the beginning of the Empire. The most notable of these was the Legion of the Vistula. Before the Battle of Eylau, Napoleon spent a few days in Warsaw, where a Polish guard of honour for him had been formed spontaneously. Attracted by the appearance and spirit of this group, the Emperor decided to incorporate a unit of Polish cavalry in his Guard.

An Imperial decree of 6 April 1807 stated that to be admitted to the regiment, an applicant had to furnish his own horse, as well as its equipment and harness. Napoleon had insisted that all members of the regiment should come from the petty nobility, since he knew they were numerous and, for that reason, he believed that he would be able to count on their pride, courage and sense of duty. Furthermore, they would all know how to ride, ensuring that their schooling proceeded rapidly – or so he hoped.

The regiment took the name *Chevau-légers Polonais*. On 28 August, Davout reported to the Emperor that its four squadrons were manned entirely by nobles, except for the trumpeters, who were French, and the *ouvriers*

(boot-makers, tailors, etc). The regiment's two majors, the captain-instructor, the two adjutant-majors, the quartermaster-treasurer and the surgeon were also French. Napoleon chose as its chief Count Vincent Corvin Krasinski, a man of limited military experience, who none the less remained its commander until he led the regiment back to Poland in 1814.

Clearly, it was necessary to shore up Krasinski with senior French officers, and it was the regiment's great good fortune that a lieutenant-colonel of the *Gendarmerie d'Élite* of the Guard, Baron Dautancourt, was one of the officers given that responsibility. Named *major en second*, he served as the regiment's organiser and instructor. His professional qualities and the confidence that he inspired in the troopers eventually won him the title of *Papa du régiment*. When, in 1814, it came time for the regiment to make its sorrowful way back to Poland, Krasinski begged the then General Dautancourt to go with them, saying, 'General, why will you not accompany such a splendid regiment, in which you are so beloved?' Dautancourt's reply was simple: 'Prince, I'm French.' However, in time, Poland was able to take possession of Dautancourt's mortal remains, which were interred in the grounds of Krasinski's estate.

What did it mean to an officer or soldier of the Guard to belong to that most prestigious body? Perquisites of membership were considerable, above and beyond the distinction afforded by simply being a part of it. These advantages and benefits undoubtedly inspired countless men in Line regiments to strive for distinction on the battlefield in the hope that their deeds would open a path to that highly favoured corps.

For a start, entrance into the Guard, for officers and men, was at a grade higher than their existing grade in a Line regiment. The Guard had its own paymaster, and pay could be as much as double that distributed to equivalent ranks in the Line. For example, the monthly pay of a colonel of the Guard Foot Grenadiers was 750 francs, whereas his Line equivalent drew 416.66 francs. A Guard sergeant-major's daily pay was 2.66 francs, while his Line opposite number received .80 francs. (In general, however, these financial benefits did not extend to members of the Middle and Young Guard regiments and squadrons, who received Line pay.) Even within the Guard, pay for equivalent ranks differed somewhat: a Foot Grenadier or Foot Chasseur officer's monthly pay came to 300 francs, while a cavalry captain drew 333.33 francs.

A striking instance that demonstrates how the Guard was offered benefits beyond those accorded to Line regiments can be found in an Imperial decree of 20 September 1805. This prescribed that:

– all soldiers of the Imperial Guard, including the *vélites*, would have the rank of sergeant or *maréchal-des-logis*, in accordance with the arm in which they served, provided that they had already completed five years' service, either in the Imperial Guard or in their previous Line regiment.
– all corporals or *brigadiers* of the Guard would have the rank of sergeant-major or *maréchal-des-logis-chef*.
– all *fourriers*, sergeants and *maréchaux-des-logis* of the Guard would have the rank of *adjutant sous-officier*.
– all sergeants-major and *maréchaux-des-logis-chefs* of the Guard would have the rank of *sous-lieutenants*.

On 19 March 1813 the Minister of War published a similar order, providing the same promotions for enlisted men, but this time extending promotions to officers as well, so that:

– *lieutenants en second* would be *lieutenants en premier*.
– *lieutenants en premier* would become *capitaines*.
– *capitaines* would become *chefs de bataillon* or *d'escadron*.
– *chefs de bataillon* or *d'escadron* would become majors.
– majors would become colonels.

In fact, this second 'all-hands' promotion may have been prompted by the need to replenish every level of the command structure of the Guard to compensate for the massive blood-letting it had suffered during the Russian campaign, rather than simply being a reward for hard service and a morale booster.

The quality of uniforms, their form and decoration were superior to those worn by the remainder of the army, and they were correspondingly more expensive. For example, outfitting a *Chasseur à cheval* of the Guard was reckoned to cost 951.96 francs, as opposed to the 300 francs for a *grenadier à pied* of the Line. Although officers of the Guard received uniform allowances, these hardly covered the cost of the brilliant attire worn even by junior officers, some of whom were forced into debt to meet those expenses.

In some respects, even the Guard's weapons were of superior quality. For example, the fittings on Guard muskets and carbines were of brass, rather than steel. The personal appearance of its troops was made distinctive by the requirement for clubbed and powdered hair, and in some regiments, the wearing of golden ear-rings.

There were other Guard practices that separated its members from their comrades-in-arms of the Line. All Guard officers, NCOs and soldiers could exercise command over their Line equivalents in rank or grade. No officer, NCO or soldier could enter the Guard unless he had ten years of service and had fought in several campaigns. In the Old Guard, all addressed one another as '*Monsieur*'. Officers and NCOs would always address a junior in that fashion. Soldiers didn't *tutoyer* (thee and thou) one another unless they were close friends. To address a close friend as '*vous*' would be construed as an insult.

Ranks that did not exist in the remainder of the army – *colonel-major* for instance – were created to fit the special requirements of the Guard. The actual ranks of the commanders of Guard cavalry regiments were almost always superior to their nominal title of 'colonel'. Four marshals, as *colonels-généraux*, were the commanders of the original four components of the Guard: foot grenadiers, Marshal Davout; foot chasseurs, Marshal Soult; cavalry, Marshal Bessières; artillery and sailors, Marshal Mortier.

The title *colonel-général* soon became purely honorary, however. Soult and Davout never commanded the Guard in the field, although Mortier did on occasion. After 1806, Bessières commanded the Guard on several occasions – in Poland in 1807 and, for a time, in Spain in 1809. His fame derives more from his role as its cavalry commander and as a corps commander.

A requirement imposed upon Line regiments, which must have caused some resentment, provided that when a Guard unit and a Line regiment encountered one another en route, the latter would give way to the Guardsmen, form up along the side of the road *en bataille* and render honour to the Guard unit by presenting arms and dipping flags, while its drums and trumpets sounded '*Aux Champs*'. The Guard detachment would return the honour without interrupting its march.

The irritation caused among the Line regiments by the many prerogatives granted to the Guard by Napoleon, and by his obvious favouritism towards its members, was offset in fair measure, however, by the image that the Guard projected. The appearance of the Guard on a field of battle invariably had a daunting psychological impact on Napoleon's adversaries. At the same time, its mere presence had a reassuring and steadying effect on other units of the French Army.

Napoleon's determination to retain the foot regiments of the Old Guard as his ultimate reserve resulted in those regiments rarely being committed to battle. He was less reluctant, however, to throw his Guard cavalry into the fray.

The primary mission of the *Gendarmerie d'Élite* of the Imperial Guard was one of public security, with particular respect to ensuring the safety of the Emperor's 'palace', rather than playing the traditional role of cavalry. For that reason, it was referred to by other men of the Guard as 'The Immortals'. Some in the army applied that caustic term to the Guard as a whole, but this would have been grossly unfair in the case of the Guard cavalry. (Intent on absolving the *Gendarmerie* of the stigma, in 1807 Napoleon did employ elements of the regiment in combat, and in each instance, they performed their duty creditably.)

By contrast, beginning in 1809 the infantry regiments of the Young Guard were pitched into practically every battle, almost as rapidly as they were formed. In most instances, they performed heroically and successfully.

Throughout its existence, the Imperial Guard continued to grow in strength and in the variety of its formations, many of them created anew. At the time of its formation in 1804, the Guard's approximate strength was 9800 men. By the time of the Russian campaign in 1812, it had grown to 56,000. Paradoxically, after that disastrous misadventure the numbers of the Guard continued to swell. They reached a total of 112,500 in 1814, as Napoleon created regiment after regiment in the Young Guard in his attempt to field sufficient forces to cut the Allied noose tightening around France. In 1804, the Guard made up a tenth of the army; by 1814, it provided between a quarter and a third of the *Grande Armée*.

Napoleon consistently tried to keep the strength of the Guard from his enemies. Faced with an acute manpower shortage at one point, he exclaimed in frustration that he couldn't simply 'stamp new regiments out of the ground'. None the less, metaphorically that is what he did, by absorbing ever younger recruits into the newly created regiments. The *Pupilles*, for example, was a regiment created in 1811 from orphans whose fathers had been killed in action.

It would seem that Napoleon scoured his imagination for titles to describe these new formations. *Tirailleurs-*

Grenadiers and *Tirailleurs-Chasseurs* were joined with *Flanqueur-Grenadiers* and *Flanqueur-Chasseurs* in the ranks of the Guard. One is reminded of Polonius describing to Hamlet the types of dramas in the repertory of the Players: '...pastoral-comical, historical-pastoral, tragical-historical, tragical-comical-historical-pastoral,' and so forth.

Regardless of their impressive-sounding titles, when all was said and done these Young Guard regiments were likely to be employed on the battlefield simply as Line infantry – and usually pretty good infantry at that. Perhaps their rather meaningless designations gave the young conscripts a sense of being part of something special, as indeed they were.

For the psychological benefit of the veteran regiments of the Guard, and of those regiments added to it during the apogee of the Empire's glory, Napoleon classified its units as Old Guard, Middle Guard and Young Guard. Initially, officers and NCOs for newly created regiments were drawn from Old Guard formations, and later from the Middle Guard. When thus assigned, such individuals retained the rank and pay, as well as the uniforms, of their original regiments.

Vélite squadrons were essential elements of Guard regiments from their creation. They were formed by physically fit, passably educated young men who aspired to become officers and who were willing to serve with the Guard, in a sort of cadet status, at their parents' expense. For this privilege, the latter paid 300 francs a year for a cavalryman or artilleryman, and 200 francs for an infantryman. If the payments stopped, in the absence of extenuating circumstances, the *vélite* would be sent to a Line regiment. In peacetime, the *vélites* were given classroom instruction in general subjects.

The *vélite* squadrons were regarded as 'nurseries' for officers of Line regiments. After three years' service, a *vélite* would be tested to determine whether he was qualified for junior officer rank in the Line, or whether he should be retained in the Guard as a private or corporal. If he had distinguished himself by exemplary conduct and zeal, he could be admitted to the Guard without full qualifications. On campaign, *vélite* squadrons were distributed among the Old Guard squadrons of their parent regiments. Any surplus would be used to form a fifth squadron.

During the early years of the Empire, the standard cavalry regiment comprised four *escadrons*, each of two *compagnies*, which were further divided into two *pelotons* (platoons) or *sections*. In 1806, this arrangement was changed to give each of the three existing Guard cavalry regiments a *vélite* squadron. As the Guard grew in size, the number of squadrons to a regiment was increased until, in some cases, a regiment would include ten or more *escadrons*.

Perhaps it is natural to assume that a cavalry regiment comprised its officers, its NCOs, its troopers, some trumpeters and a standard bearer or two. In fact, the structure of a French cavalry regiment was not unlike that of a small village. After 1806, its *état-major* (staff) would include:

1   *colonel-commandant*
2   *majors*
5   *chefs d'escadron* – 1 of a *vélite* of a squadron

1   *chef d'escadron instructeur*
1   *quartier-maître-trésorier*
1   *capitaine instructeur*
2   *adjutants-major* – 1 of a *vélite* squadron
5   *sous-adjutants-major* – 1 of a *vélite* squadron
4   *porte-étendards*
2   *aides-artiste-vétérinaire* – 1 a *vélite* (senior veterinarians)
1   *adjutant-lieutenant pour les vivres* (food supplies)
1   *adjutant-lieutenant pour les fourrages* (horse feed)
1   *adjutant-lieutenant pour l'habillement* (uniforms)
5   *officiers de santé* – 2 of 1st class; 3 of 2nd and 3rd class
1   *trompette-major*
3   *brigadier-trompettes* – 1 a *vélite*
1   *timbalier*
1   *maître-tailleur* (master tailor)
1   *maître-culottier* (master trouser-maker)
1   *maître-bottier* (master boot-maker)
1   *sous-instructeur-maréchal-des-logis-chef*
1   *vaguemestre-maréchal-des-logis-chef* (chief baggage master)
2   *artistes-vétérinaire* – 1 a *vélite*
1   *maître armurier* (master armourer)
1   *maître sellier* (master saddle-maker)
1   *maître éperonnier* (master spur-maker)
2   *maréchaux-ferrant* (sergeant-farriers)

Each company of Grenadiers or Chasseurs would have:

1   *capitaine*
2   *lieutenants en premier*
2   *lieutenants en second*
1   *maréchal-des-logis-chef*
6   *maréchaux-des-logis*
1   *fourrier*
10   *brigadiers*
96   *grenadiers* or *chasseurs*
3   *trompettes*
1   *maréchal-ferrant*.

Colonels of the regiments were likely to have the actual rank of *général de brigade*, or higher, in which case they would receive the benefits of that rank. (At one point, the actual rank of the Chasseurs' colonel was *général de division*, and his *colonel en premier* and *colonel en second* were both *généraux de brigade*.)

After the campaign of 1805, Napoleon decided that Guard cavalry regiments of five squadrons – 1000 men – were too large to be handled effectively in battle by one officer. Consequently, on 15 April 1806, he decreed that, on campaign, such regiments were to be divided into two *régiments de marche*, each commanded by one of the regiment's two majors, both subordinate to the orders of the parent regiment's colonel. The resulting formations were designated, for example, 1st and 2nd Chasseurs, etc. The same decree prescribed that when a squadron was detached for independent service and would be absent for several days, it would be fleshed out to 250 men by the addition of fifty *vélites*.

En route, Guard cavalry regiments marched at a steady pace of 6 km/h, with ten-minute stops every hour. When passing over hard or stony ground, or under icy conditions, the men dismounted and walked their horses.

Guard cavalry regiments had two primary roles: they served as a bodyguard for the Emperor; and they constituted a formidable reserve striking force under his direct and sole command, which he employed at critical stages of a battle. In addition, the light cavalry regiments performed scouting, screening and advance post duties.

The first role was set out in great detail by a series of decrees and orders, which were followed meticulously throughout the Empire. The four *colonels-généraux* of the Guard took in turn, on a weekly basis, the duty of being constantly in attendance upon Napoleon. In the palace, they occupied rooms near his, and in the field, they slept in his tent. (This responsibility was delegated to lesser luminaries when the four marshals became corps commanders.) At all times, whether in Paris or in the field, each of the Guard cavalry regiments furnished a duty squadron to remain in the general area of the Emperor's headquarters. When the Guard was in Paris, the duty squadrons were rotated every three months. One of the duty squadrons, on rotation, was required to remain in the Emperor's immediate vicinity.

When Napoleon left his headquarters on horseback, the four duty squadrons rode at a considerable distance – usually about 1000 m – behind him. Sometimes, however, when he set out without giving any notice, the Chasseurs of the picket alone would be hard pressed to keep up with him, as happened at Malojaroslavets during the retreat from Moscow.

It is in their second role, however, that the Guard cavalry regiments are most often portrayed – officers leading their troopers in a flat-out charge, trumpets blaring and standards streaming in the wind. Rousselot has painted a number of such scenes, although they are on a more intimate scale than the sweeping canvases of Detaille or Meissonier, since his focus is on the uniforms worn by the men who carried out such charges.

As circumstances and terrain permitted, a squadron charge would be carried out in a straight, compact line, in accordance with carefully defined principles. At a distance of 200–300 m from the enemy, one of the squadron's two companies would form up in two ranks, each of 40–48 men. The remaining company would form in the rear as a reserve. At the command, '*Escadrons, en avant – marche!*', the two ranks would move forward at a walking pace.

Half-way to the enemy position, at the command, '*Au trot!*', the troopers would draw their sabres and urge their horses into a trot. Almost immediately, the command, '*Au galop!*', would be given.

At 60 m from the enemy, the commander would call out, '*Chargez!*', and the trumpeters would sound the charge. The troopers would rise in their stirrups and go to a full gallop. Each of the men in the first rank would extend his sabre, the point a little lower than his hand, held at the height of his eyes, and the cutting edge of the blade to the right. Meanwhile, troopers in the second rank would raise their sabres above their heads, points toward the rear and slightly higher than their fists.

These tactics prevented the men's horses from becoming blown at the outset of combat and permitted each rank to be kept reasonably straight. After the shock of the initial collision, the riders of the first rank would separate, allowing the second to deliver another blow to the enemy.

If the entire regiment was charging in a line abreast of squadrons, each *chef d'escadron* would be at the head of his respective squadron. The regiment's colonel would be at the head of the squadron where he believed his presence would be most effective. The regiment's *colonel en second* would remain close to his colonel, unless the latter deemed it desirable for him to lead another squadron.

When the charge was sounded, the officers riding in advance of the first rank would ease up so that the croups of their horses were among that rank, the men directly behind them falling back to permit this.

The trumpeters would remain slightly to the rear of the second rank, the trumpet-major at their head, unless the colonel directed the latter to stay close to him. A trumpeter could only sound his calls easily when his horse was standing or walking. At a trot, much less a gallop, the use of a trumpet became much more difficult. Then, the trumpeter would rise in his stirrups, lean slightly forward, his trumpet pointed downward, to the right of his mount's neck and braced against it to prevent sudden shocks, which might have caused serious injury to his mouth.

Opinion as to the correct moment for the men to draw their sabres differed among experienced cavalry commanders. Keeping troopers standing for extended periods with their sabres drawn and resting on their shoulders, while waiting to go into action, put a strain on their arms and wrists. Conversely, it was reasoned that having the men draw their sabres when the order to trot was given raised their spirits, and startled and intimidated the enemy.

The act of drawing a sabre had the additional benefit that it caused the rider's thighs to contract against his horse's flanks. This sensation, combined with the rasp of the blade as it was drawn from its scabbard, encouraged the animal to gather itself for the charge.

A charge could be executed either in successive waves by squadrons, or in a line of squadrons. If the enemy line had been broken by the charge, a call was sounded immediately to rally the men to the standard. At the same time, detachments of the squadron would be ordered to pursue the broken elements of the enemy to prevent them from regrouping.

The responsibility for performing the secondary duties of the Guard cavalry most often fell to the *Chevau-légers Polonais*, who had been trained initially in the techniques of advance-guard and outpost operations in Spain by the renowned light cavalry general, Count Antoine Charles Louis Lasalle. Although they had not fully absorbed their instructions by the time the regiment's first squadron started up the road to the pass of Somosierra, by the third, and successful, attempt to carry out the Emperor's order to clear the road, they had learned a painful lesson, which would stand them in good stead from then on.

To follow in detail the many feats of arms performed by the four illustrious Guard cavalry regiments is beyond the scope and intent of this volume. However, a brief account of the part they played during the campaigns of the Napoleonic armies in Austria, Spain, Germany, Poland and Russia, in the Campaign of France, and finally at Waterloo, should give the reader a greater appreciation of the extraordinary achievements of the resolute soldiers whom Rousselot has so skillfully created in these remarkable paintings.

I believe that even the most dispassionate reader of the accounts of the fifty major battles and lesser engagements in which the men of these regiments participated, in the course of some eleven years, must wonder at the degree to which they almost invariably dominated their opponents by a combination of psychology, reckless courage and fearless determination to outdo themselves whenever the Emperor challenged them to do so. But that story has been related many times elsewhere. For the purposes of this volume, it is sufficient to follow, in outline, the course of the campaigns in which the regiments participated, briefly recounting a few of their more memorable feats of arms, which are embedded within the Napoleonic legend.

As the Imperial Guard was inaugurated in May 1804, Napoleon had at his disposal two cavalry regiments composed of officers and men who had previously won laurels under his command, but with somewhat less 'glittering' titles. It would not be long, however, before the *Chasseurs à cheval* and the *Grenadiers à cheval de la Garde Impériale* would be called upon to demonstrate that, with their new, more grandiose style, they were every bit as formidable a weapon in the hands of the Emperor as they had been for the First Consul – or even more so.

After defeating Mack at Ulm, Napoleon had ordered Murat to take Walther's dragoons and d'Hautpoul's cuirassiers to pursue the withdrawing Austrians. On 20 November, at Olmütz, Murat's force ran up against 6000 Russian cavalrymen, and Walther's dragoons and a light cavalry brigade, under Lasalle, were pushed back. Murat struck back with d'Hautpoul's division to restore the situation. Napoleon sent Bessières with the Chasseurs and Grenadiers to Murat's assistance. Bessières formed the Guard squadrons into two lines: three squadrons of Grenadiers and two of Chasseurs, the second line in reverse. The second line was to attack only if the first line was repulsed.

The attack of the Guard squadrons, added to the weight of the cuirassiers, drove off the Russian cavalry, who left their light artillery in French hands. There was no need for the second line to attack.

A notable example of the daring enterprise and fearless aggressiveness displayed by junior officers of these regiments is afforded by the actions of Lieutenant Desmichels of the Chasseurs a day later. His regiment, still a part of Murat's force, had caught up with the tail of the fleeing Austrians outside Nürnberg. Desmichels, leading a platoon of thirty Chasseurs as the point of the advance guard, immediately attacked the 300 men of a light infantry regiment forming the Austrian rearguard. When they surrendered, Desmichels pressed on, capturing another 400 men and two flags.

At that point, the colonel of the La Tour dragoons, the best heavy cavalry regiment of the Austrian army, led 500 men of his regiment to the aid of their countrymen. Desmichels had only about two dozen men left at that stage, but observing that the dragoons were having difficulty in deploying, he attacked the leading platoon, driving them back on the following troops. Then the squadrons of the Chasseurs and some *carabiniers* came to his support, completing the rout of the Austrians. In all, 150 of the dragoons, including their colonel, were captured. When the Chasseurs rejoined the Emperor's field headquarters a week later, Napoleon made Desmichels a captain and a *Légionnaire*.

The first major battle in which Guard cavalry regiments participated was Austerlitz, on 2 December 1805. A brief account of their achievements on that occasion will be found elsewhere in this volume. It was at Eylau, on 8 February 1807, that the Grenadiers and the Chasseurs made important contributions to that hard-won victory.

Early 1808 saw the regiments separated. The newest, the *Chevau-légers Polonais*, and one squadron each from the Grenadiers, the Chasseurs and the Dragoons, together with a platoon of the Mameluks, headed for Spain under General Lepic, as part of Murat's command. There, in May, the Chasseurs and Mameluks succeeded, with difficulty, in extricating themselves from the mob during the revolt in Madrid; at Somosierra, the Poles won, at considerable cost, a reputation for reckless courage.

With the Austrian campaign scheduled to get under way in April 1809, early that year most of the Guard elements that had been in Spain returned to France with Napoleon. The *Chevau-légers Polonais*, under the overall command of Krasinski, had been divided into a brigade of two regiments. Delaître commanded one, and Dautancourt, the other. The latter also remained second-in-command of the brigade.

At Wagram, Pierre Daumesnil, one of the Chasseur *chefs d'escadron*, had lost a leg – his 23rd wound. When he recovered, Napoleon appointed him governor of the fortress of Vincennes in Paris. When, in 1814, he was called upon by the Allies to surrender the fortress, he replied, 'When you return the leg you have taken from me, I shall turn over the fortress to you. In the meanwhile, I advise you to keep clear of my guns, which are loaded.' History does not reveal how that stand-off was resolved.

In January 1810, the squadrons of the *Chevau-légers Polonais* – by then, having added '*lanciers*' to their title – were separated, two of them returning to Spain, while the others remained in Paris, their men serving in a duty squadron periodically, working on their French with some private tutelage, and otherwise enjoying the pleasures of garrison duty in the capital. Two squadrons of Dragoons and successive squadrons of the Chasseurs accompanied their comrades to Spain. It would be March 1812 before most of these men returned to France.

The type of counter-guerrilla operations conducted by the Polish squadrons in Spain exposed them to the entire range of Goya's *Disasters of War*. The pitiless form of warfare seemed to bear little relevance to their aspirations for a free Poland, and they may have felt that it was not what they had signed on for. Thus it was with an enormous sense of relief that the 315 Polish Light Horse Lancers of those two squadrons were able to rejoin the body of the regiment in Paris. Some were given the task of training the newly formed Second Regiment in the use of the lance.

The spring of 1812 saw the Guard, along with the rest of the army and France's allied contingents, preparing for what Napoleon described in an Imperial proclamation of 22 June – the day before the crossing of the Niemen began – as 'the second Polish war'. In March, General Lefèbvre-

Desnouëttes – who had been captured by the British at Benavente in 1808, and then, violating his parole, had made his way clandestinely to France early in 1812 – had resumed command of the Chasseurs. The regiment started the campaign with five squadrons, all Old Guard, plus the Mameluks. They would not be called upon to participate in the battles of Smolensk or Borodino, although they always provided Napoleon's personal escort. The campaign cost the Chasseurs 500 men.

In March, under the command of Bonardi de Saint-Sulpice, the Dragoons set out on the long road to Russia. On 10 August, they were joined by a detachment from Spain. Of the sixty-four officers and 1022 men who took part in the campaign, only half returned. Because of their familiarity with the territory and their knowledge of Russian, the Poles were much in demand for a variety of missions during the campaign, but their losses were no less significant.

The remnants of the Guard were at Königsberg by Christmas Day 1812, and by mid-January 1813, the remaining Horse Guards had arrived at the depots established by Bessières outside Posen. There were 125 Polish Lancers, 260 Chasseurs, 120 Dragoons and 127 Grenadiers.

As the reconstruction of the army began in January, Napoleon decreed that each Guard cavalry regiment would be expanded to become a brigade, consisting of one Old Guard and one Young Guard regiment. Thus the Chasseur brigade would consist of ten squadrons of 250 men each. The first five squadrons, plus the Mameluks as the tenth, were designated Old Guard and known as *premiers Chasseurs*. Squadrons six to nine were Young Guard and called *seconds Chasseurs*. Lefèbvre-Desnouëttes had as his *commandant en second Général de division* Guyot, and as *colonels-majors*, Lion for the Old Guard and Meuziau for the Young Guard.

Chevalier Kirmann commanded the tenth squadron (Mameluks), which had been increased in strength to two companies, totalling 250 men. The first company had been formed from the cadre of the original squadron, plus troopers chosen from cavalry of the Line. They were designated *premier Mameluks* and were given Mameluk pay. The second company consisted of men selected from those who had been offered to the Chasseurs by the Departments of the Empire. They were designated *seconds Mameluks* and received Line cavalry pay. The regiment's Old Guard squadrons were made up of one-third survivors of the Russian campaign and two-thirds troopers from Spain. Almost all of the 1st Regiment had been awarded the Star of the Legion, and a number had also received the Order of the Iron Crown.

A new call for men allowed five Dragoon squadrons to be brought up to strength, plus the formation of a sixth, designated as the 2nd Regiment, or 2nd Dragoons, its men being called Young Guard *cavaliers seconds*. *Général de division* Count Ornano had replaced General Saint-Sulpice as *Colonel-commandant*, and had *Général de brigade* Letort as *colonel-major* and Lieutenant-colonel Testot-Ferry as the *Chef d'escadron* for the sixth squadron.

The Grenadiers' four original Old Guard squadrons were replenished, while fifth and sixth Young Guard squadrons were added to form the second regiment, its men also being called *cavaliers seconds*. Their *Colonel-commandant* was *Général de division* Count Walther,

who had as his majors *Général de division* Baron Laferrière-Lévêque and *Général* Baron Castex.

The Polish – by then, the 1st *Chevau-légers lanciers* – were organised by Dautancourt at a strength of 1500, comprising survivors from Russia, 500 men from Dombrowski's division and a few others, mostly from the Third Guard Lancers. He kept for himself the Old Guard companies assigned exclusively as the Emperor's escort, while the other nine companies were designated 2nd Lancers, under that great survivor General Count Krasinski, and attached to Lefèbvre-Desnouëttes.

By early April the Guard cavalry, under the command of Marshal Bessières, was on its way to Gotha. It was organised in a light cavalry division, under Lefèbvre-Desnouëttes, and a heavy division, under Ornano. On 2 May, the first battle of the campaign took place at Lützen. Although it was a French victory, albeit an indecisive one, its prelude cost the life of one of Napoleon's finest soldiers when Bessières was struck by a ricocheting cannon-ball at Rippach, while carrying out a reconnaissance near enemy lines on the previous day. Three weeks later, at Bautzen, Napoleon would lose another old and valued friend when Grand Marshal Duroc was fatally wounded by another Russian cannon-ball. This experience prompted Napoleon to reiterate an earlier order, directing the dispersal of his suite on battlefields.

In the final stage of the battle, both of Lefèbvre-Desnouëttes' Guard Lancer regiments, the Chasseurs and the Mameluks, helped drive the Russians from the field. An armistice on 4 June brought the spring campaign to an abrupt close.

In August 1813, the organisation of the Guard cavalry, then 8000 strong and under a new commander, Nansouty, was as follows:

1st Division, commanded by Count Ornano: Berg Lancers, Edouard Colbert's 2nd *Chevau-légers lanciers*, Pinteville's Young Guard *Dragons*.

2nd Division, commanded by Lefèbvre-Desnouëttes: Krasinski's Young Guard squadrons of *Chevau-légers Polonais*, *Chasseurs* and Castex's *Grenadiers à cheval*.

3rd Division, commanded by Walther: Old Guard squadrons of Lion's *Chasseurs*, Letort's *Dragons* and Laferrière-Lévêque's *Grenadiers à cheval*.

The armistice was broken by mid-August, and the interrupted Leipzig campaign was resumed with yet another hollow victory, at Dresden on 26/27 August – hollow, because losses suffered by three of his lieutenants on separate battlefields disrupted Napoleon's strategic plans. In the course of the battle, two squadrons of Polish Lancers distinguished themselves by putting to rout a Prussian hussar regiment and capturing its commander, Colonel Blücher, a relative of 'the' Blücher. This earned for *Chef d'escadron* Jankowski a star of the Legion.

On the third day of the 'Battle of Nations' at Leipzig, on 18 October, Napoleon gave the Dragoons' commander, Letort, four squadrons – each of 250 Chasseurs, Dragoons, Grenadiers and 2nd Regiment Lancers – and ordered him to disperse the elite Austrian La Tour dragoon regiment. This Letort and his men proceeded to do, capturing 200 of the Austrian cavalrymen. Among the Guard's losses that day was Assistant Adjutant-major Guindey of the Horse Grenadiers, who was remembered for having killed Prince Louis of Prussia at Saalfeld.

But the gravest loss was that of Prince Poniatowski,

who had been made a marshal on the evening before he drowned, wounded and attempting to swim his horse across the Elster after the bridge to Lindenau had been prematurely blown up. This was a grievous blow to the Polish Lancers, for whom the Prince had personified their hopes for the freedom of their land. They asked Krasinski to request a meeting for them with Napoleon, which he did reluctantly. Napoleon's appeal to them won over the perplexed men, and they continued to do their best for him and their second *patrie*.

On 30 October, at Hanau, the *Grande Armée*, retreating from Leipzig, encountered a force of some 43,000 Bavarians, Austrians and cossacks under Wrede, who repulsed the initial French attempt to break through their blockade of the road to France. Soon, however, Napoleon arrived with the Guard artillery, cavalry and infantry, and resumed the attack. A detachment of the Polish Lancers, led by Jerzmanowski, launched themselves against the Bavarians. Almost immediately, they were joined by the remainder of the regiment and the other Guard squadrons, supported by the artillery. The Allied force was routed. Nansouty was so pleased with the Polish Lancers' dispatch of the Bavarian cavalry that he told Colonel Dautancourt that he might consider himself promoted to *général de brigade* on the spot; this was made official a month later.

Operations in Saxony during 1813 had made Napoleon realise that it was imperative to find a means of dealing with the constant harassment of his troops by cossack formations. After considering various solutions to the problem, in December of that year he set out the organisation of the Guard cavalry for the campaign of 1814, at the same time creating three regiments of *Eclaireurs* (scouts), each of four squadrons of 250 men apiece. The first regiment of *Eclaireurs-Grenadiers* would be attached to the *Grenadiers à cheval*; the second regiment of *Eclaireurs-Dragons* would operate with the *Dragons de l'Impératrice*; and the third regiment of *Eclaireurs-Lanciers* would be associated with the *1er Chevau-légers lanciers Polonais*.

At the time, the *1er Lanciers* – as the Polish Lancers were referred to in official documents – consisted of fourteen companies, divided into two regiments. The first was Old Guard (1st to 6th companies), the second, Middle Guard (7th to 12th companies); the 13th and 14th companies were Young Guard.

On 10 January 1814, General Count de Nansouty again took command of the cavalry of the Guard. By 26 January, it was organised into the 1st Division (light cavalry), under General Lefèbvre-Desnouëttes; the 2nd Division (light cavalry), under General Edouard Colbert; and the 3rd Division (heavy cavalry), under General Guyot.

At Berry-au-Bac, on 5 March, Napoleon ordered Nansouty to seize the critically important bridge over the Aisne. The Guard cavalry and two regiments of Polish Lancers of the Line, under General Pac, who had just joined up with the Guard, attacked the cossacks protecting the bridge, putting them to flight and capturing a number of prisoners. Among these was a Prince Gagarine, who loudly denied his identity.

The Battle of Craonne, on 6/7 March, proved a costly and fruitless victory for the rapidly dwindling French forces. Once again, the Guard cavalry brigade, led by General Laferrière-Lévêque until a shell carried off one of his legs, played a key role in the hard-fought defeat of the Allied force. Colonel Testot-Ferry, at the head of his 1st *Eclaireurs-Grenadiers*, took command of the cavalry after Laferrière-Lévêque's injury, leading the Guard squadrons right over the Russian artillery to seize and retain the heights of Craonne. On the battlefield, Napoleon decorated several of the *Eclaireurs*, and awarded Testot-Ferry the title of Baron of the Empire.

When the succeeding Battle of Laon proved indecisive, Napoleon withdrew his forces to Soissons. Almost all of his generals were wounded, among them Nansouty, who was forced to give up his command on the day after Craonne. He was replaced by General Sébastiani. Colbert was still at the head of the 1st Division, Exelmans had taken the place of Guyot with the 2nd, and Letort had been given provisional command of the 3rd, replacing the wounded Laferrière-Lévêque.

Again, the composition of the Guard cavalry was modified:

1st Division, under General Colbert: 1st and 2nd Lancers of the Line, General Pac; 2nd Regiment of *Chevau-légers lanciers*; six Polish artillery cannon.

2nd Division, under General Exelmans: 1st Regiment of *Chevau-légers lanciers*; 3rd Regiment of *Eclaireurs-Lanciers*; *Dragons de l'Impératrice*; 2nd Regiment of *Eclaireurs-Dragons*.

3rd Division, under General Letort: *Chasseurs à cheval*; *Grenadiers à cheval*; 1st Regiment of *Eclaireurs-Grenadiers*.

On the 12th, the Russian and Prussian troops of the corps commanded by the emigré French General Saint-Priest, which had occupied Rheims, were driven from the city by a surprise attack led by an *Eclaireur* regiment, in the course of which Saint-Priest was killed. On the 17th Napoleon left Rheims, the strength of his cavalry reduced to some 3000 sabres, and his entire army numbering no more than 23,000 combatants. Craonne and Laon had cost him about 12,000 men.

There followed a succession of almost daily skirmishes, culminating in a major engagement at Arcis-sur-Aube on 20 March, where the French force of some 20,000 men confronted the entire Allied Army of Bohemia. Ordered forward by Sébastiani, the divisions led by Exelmans and Colbert collided with masses of Austrian, Russian and Bavarian cavalry and they were driven back. At one point, Napoleon was forced to shelter in a square formed by the Legion of the Vistula until the infantry of the Old and Young Guard could stabilise the situation.

The Guard cavalry, by then reduced to 1600 men, received timely support when General Lefèbvre-Desnouëttes arrived from Versailles with 1500 reinforcements and took over the command of his division. In the combat at Saint-Dizier on 26 March, Napoleon himself, sword in hand, led a charge of the Guard against the cavalry of Wintzingerode, during which other *Eclaireurs* also distinguished themselves.

Meanwhile, Schwarzenberg's army was closing in on Paris, and on 30 March he launched his 145,000 men in an attack on the city. On the 28th, General Ornano, in command of the Guard cavalry units at that time in their regimental depots, had gathered together ten small squadrons of Grenadiers, Dragoons, *Chevau-légers*, Chasseurs, Mameluks and *Eclaireurs* – perhaps 800 men

– and placed them under the command of General Dautancourt.

On the 29th, a detachment of the 3rd *Eclaireurs* had fought their final battle at Claye. A second detachment of their regiment had been sent to escort the Empress, who was leaving Paris. Dautancourt was left with 330 men to aid in the defence of Paris.

After a skirmish with cossacks at le Bourget, and a futile attempt to establish a defensive position on the Butte Montmartre, on the 30th Dautancourt and his men learned that the city had been surrendered to the enemy. At dawn on the 31st, a detachment of the *Eclaireurs* was sent to blow up a bridge at Choisy-le-Roi. That was the last action of the *3ème Régiment d'Eclaireurs de la Garde Impériale*. Dautancourt led what was left of his brigade to Fontainebleau.

Relieved by Napoleon of their oath of fidelity to him, the Poles of the regiment were united with other Polish troops assembled at Saint-Denis under General Krasinski; by early June, they were on their way back to Poland, where Krasinski would put them at the disposition of Emperor Alexander. In his historical notes, General Dautancourt often observed that, during the campaign of 1814, the *Chevau-légers Polonais* and the 3rd *Eclaireurs* virtually formed a single regiment.

Having returned to Paris from Elba on 20 March 1815 – the King and his household having hastily decamped the night before – Napoleon declared on the 22nd that, 'The Imperial Guard's functions and privileges are hereby restored.' There followed an intensive effort to locate what was left of the regiments that had been converted into elements of the Royal Guard, and to reconstitute them as Imperial regiments. Soon the Grenadiers, the Chasseurs, the Dragoons and the Second *Chevau-légers* were brought together in Paris. On 8 April, Napoleon set out the organisation of the reconstituted Guard. The four cavalry regiments were each to comprise four squadrons, and Guyot, Ornano, Lefèbvre-Desnouëttes and Colbert were given command of their former regiments.

In the aftermath of Napoleon's final defeat and exile, on 3 August, the King declared the dissolution of the Guard, and the process of deactivating its regiments began. *That* Imperial Guard had ceased to exist.

The effort by Napoleon's nephew 39 years later to clothe his reign in the glory won by his uncle's Guard had something of the air of an operetta about it. Not content with one chasseur regiment, Napoleon III added to the Guard a regiment of *Guides*. The Second Empire's version of the *Grenadiers à cheval* was a regiment of *Carabiniers*, while the cuirassiers, who had remained Line regiments under Napoleon I, formed two regiments in the new Guard. The *Cent Gardes*, with their sabre bayonets, were thrown in for good measure. But no one – least of all, Bismarck – was fooled.

A final thought. Anyone finding it difficult to understand the fascination that the Napoleonic era holds for so many of us, will find in the Translator's Preface to Anne Brown's translation of Commandant Lachouque's monumental work on Napoleon and his Guard (*The Anatomy of Glory*) a more eloquent explanation of that phenomenon than I am able to provide. We are greatly indebted to them both.

GLOSSARY

Banderole cross-belt

Bonnet de police fatigue cap

Bottes à l'écuyère top-boots, riding boots

Capote overcoat

Ceinturon belt

Colback busby-style cap of fur

Contre-epaulette fringeless epaulette

Dolman sleeved, braided chasseur or hussar waistcoat

Eclaireurs scouts

En baudrier wearing a sword-belt over a shoulder and across the chest

Etat-major headquarters staff

Flamme pennon of a lance; bag of a colback; or trumpet banner

Giberne cartridge pouch

Grande tenue full dress

Grande tenue de service service full dress

Grand uniforme full dress uniform, also called *uniforme de parade*

Guérite sentry shelter

Habit dress long-tailed coat with broad lapels, collar of coat colour and contrasting round or pointed cuffs

Habit de petit uniform an undress *habit*, sometimes called *second habit*. It has plain round cuffs without the three-button slash of the dress *habit*, except for Grenadier trumpeters (*see* Plate 30)

Habit-veste a short-tailed coat with a single row of buttons, unadorned, with the waist cut straight across at the front

Konfederatka a soft cloth officer's hat with a squared Polish top and fur band at the base

Kurtka Polish short-tailed sleeved jacket with reversible plastron

Manteau capote caped overcoat

Ordonnance orderly, or officer's or NCO's personal servant from his regiment

Pantalon de voyage long trousers for travelling

Pavillon the cloth upper portion of a lancer's square-topped cap (*schapska*)

Petit uniforme undress uniform; also *petite tenue*

Planche a sheet of one or more printed images

Porte-aigle eagle-bearer

Porte-aigrette the metal holder for the horse-hair tuft at the forward edge of a dragoon's or cuirassier's helmet

Porte-étendard standard-bearer

Porte-giberne cross-belt carrying the ammunition pouch

Porte-mousqueton cross-belt from which a carbine or musket may be suspended; often joined to the *porte-giberne* by a brass rivet

Redingote a light, knee-length undress coat with full skirts worn by officers and NCOs, usually on dismounted duty in quarters

Retroussis lining of coat tails, turned back and hooked or sewn together

Revers lapels of a uniform coat

Schabraque decorated cloth covering a horse's back, beneath the saddle

Schapska (*czapska*) lancer's square-topped cap, narrowing down to the base

Surculottes overalls

Surtout an undress long-tailed coat with plain cuffs and no lapels. (Grenadier and Dragoon trumpeters' surtouts had decorated cuffs)

Tenue de campagne uniform worn on campaign

Tenue de charge field uniform

Tenue d'écurie stable dress

Tenue de parade parade uniform

Tenue de grande parade full dress parade uniform

Tenue de quartier quarters dress

Tenue de route march order

Tenue de service service dress

Tenue de société society dress

Tenue de ville walking-out dress

Tête de colonne leading unit of a column of troops, usually composed of musicians or sappers

Timbalier mounted kettledrummer

Vélites volunteer aspirant officers, financially subsidised by their families

RANKS

Cavalier trooper

Brigadier cavalry corporal

Sous-officier non-commissioned officer

Trompette-brigadier corporal trumpeter

Trompette-major trumpet-major

Fourrier quartermaster sergeant/company clerk

Maréchal-des-logis cavalry sergeant

Maréchal-des-logis-chef cavalry sergeant-major

Maréchal-ferrant sergeant farrier

Lieutenant en second second lieutenant

Lieutenant en premier first lieutenant

Capitaine captain

Chef d'escadron cavalry major, squadron commander

Colonel colonel

Colonel en second deputy commander of a regiment

Colonel en premier commander of a regiment

Général de brigade brigadier-general

Général de division major-general

Maréchal lieutenant-general; corps commander

THE PLATES

PLATE 2

Garde Impériale – Chasseurs à cheval. 1804–1815
Senior officer and junior officer. Service full dress.

The hussar-style dress uniform of the *Chasseurs à cheval* was one of the most brilliant – and most expensive – uniforms of the Guard and, therefore, of the entire Napoleonic army. The white plume and three gold chevrons on the sleeves of the pelisse and dolman of the officer in the foreground indicate that he is a major, possibly a *chef d'escadron*, and thus a member of the regimental staff. In the centre of the cockade, at the base of the plume on his colback, is a gilded eagle. He is shaking hands with a captain, whose green and red plume is identical to those of the troopers. These officers' *grande tenue de service* would be worn, for example, at the daily parades when their regiment was providing the service squadron at an Imperial residence.

Suspended from his red morocco leather belt is the major's parade sabre, the hilt and scabbard of which are of chased and gilded bronze. His richly embroidered dress sabretache bears the Imperial coat of arms, on which a gilded metal eagle is centred. The officers' pelisses are trimmed with white throat of Canadian fox fur. Their barrel sashes, passed three times around their waists, are of green wool with gold lace slides, knots, cords and tassels. Their breeches are of ochre deerskin, and their hussar-style boots are trimmed with gold braid and tassels.

From their black fur colbacks depend *flammes* (bags) of scarlet cloth, trimmed along their seams with gold cord and tipped with gold tassels. Their black leather *gibernes* (cartridge pouches), decorated with gilded metal eagles, are carried on a green leather *banderole* (cross-belt) trimmed with gold lace and ornamented with a gilded Imperial eagle and crown joined by two small chains.

Garde Impériale - Chasseurs à cheval 1804.1815.

Officier supérieur et officier subalterne, grande tenue de service.

Plate 3

Garde Impériale – Chasseurs à cheval. 1804–1815
Lieutenant eagle-bearer. 1804–1812.

The title of the lieutenant in this painting – *porte-aigle* (eagle-bearer) rather than *porte-étendard* (standard bearer) – reflects Napoleon's wish that the gilded bronze eagles presented by him to his regiments should represent the Emperor, the Nation, and the honour and spirit of their corps. They, rather than the standards which hung below them, were the symbols that were to be preserved at any cost, for the honour of the regiment and the army.

Eagle-bearers in the Guard were always subalterns. Here, the lieutenant is escorted by a *brigadier* and three troopers. He is in parade dress, a white plume on his colback denoting his place in the regimental staff. Two unusual characteristics of this eagle are noteworthy: the hunter's horn, symbolic of chasseurs, affixed to the front (and back) of the eagle's base, rather than a regimental number; and the gold wreath around the eagle's neck. After the victorious Austerlitz campaign, Parisian dignitaries proposed that the city present such gold wreaths to regiments returning to Paris. Napoleon agreed, and the Guard received their wreaths on 25 November 1807.

The flag shown is an 1804-style guidon, presented by Napoleon to his regiments on the *Champ de Mars* on 5 December 1805, when the Chasseurs and the *Grenadiers à cheval* each received two eagles. The inscription on the face of the flag read, '*L'EMPEREUR DES FRANÇAIS AU REGnt. DE CHASSEURS À CHEVAL DE LA GARDE IMPÉRIALE*'. The reverse bore a gold-crowned eagle centred in the motto, '*VALEUR ET DISCIPLINE*', below which were the letters '*Ier ESCADRON*' (or '*IIème ESCADRON*').

Garde Impériale ~ Chasseurs à cheval. 1804.1815

Lieutenant. porte - aigle 1804-1812.

PLATE 4

Garde Impériale – Chasseurs à cheval. 1804–1815
Kettledrummer and his escort. 1804–1805.

Having a colourful kettledrummer to lead the band in a parade was considered highly desirable by every cavalry regiment, and fantasy reigned in the design of their uniforms. In 1804, Bruno Lemoine was the *timbalier* for the Chasseurs, and he is shown here in his uniform *à la mameluk*. In all probability, Lemoine only appeared in this guise on very special ceremonial occasions. He held the rank of *brigadier-trompette* and, as such, normally wore the uniform of the regiment's other trumpeters. In the latter role, he was killed in 1808 at Torquemada.

The drum banners and the horse's schabraque are in the traditional chasseur colour, which is echoed in the green plumes, in the bow decorating the horse's head, and in the green and gold braiding in its mane. Mameluk-style stirrups complete the ensemble. Drum banners of this type could cost as much as 9000 francs. The *Musée de l'Armée* possesses only the central portion of Lemoine's sabretache, decorated with golden musical instruments on a crimson background.

Since Rousselot did not include an image of this kettledrummer in his four *planches* on the Chasseurs, this painting provides a significant addition to his illustrations of the men of that regiment.

By 1810, a different uniform for the *timbalier* and his horse's schabraque had appeared, possibly introduced for the occasion of Napoleon's marriage to Marie-Louise. In this new attire, the *timbalier* wore a trumpeter's hussar-style uniform, although his pelisse was scarlet, rather than the normal crimson. The drum banners and the schabraque were scarlet, being decorated with double rows of gold lace and Imperial emblems.

Garde Impériale ~ Chasseurs à cheval 1804.1815.

Le timbalier et son escorte 1804 - 1805

PLATE 5

Garde Impériale – Chasseurs à cheval. 1804–1815
Parade uniform. 1804–1815.

The chasseurs seen here wear the full dress uniforms in which they are most frequently depicted. Their trimmed and powdered hair is bound in queues with black silk ribbons, and the artist has given them the golden ear-rings worn by some Guard regiments. Their colbacks of black fur on rigid leather frames are marginally higher toward the rear than the front, and taper slightly outward toward the crown. The cord holding the two *aurore* (yellow-orange) flounders and tassels is looped around the wire that supports the cockade, in the centre of which is an embroidered eagle. A scarlet *flamme*, its seams bound with *aurore* cord and tipped with a tassel, falls over the right side of the colback. The colback's leather chin straps support brass curb-chains.

The two chevrons on the sleeves of the pelisse and the dolman of the chasseur in the foreground identify him as a *brigadier*. Both garments are decorated with five vertical rows of copper buttons, joined by lengths of *aurore* braid. His pelisse is trimmed with curled black lamb's-wool and lined with white flannel. Hungarian boots, pleated at the instep for comfort, are trimmed with *aurore* braid and tassels.

The point of the schabraque is decorated with an Imperial eagle. The horse's halter is lined with scalloped green cloth, and the snaffle-bridle is of *aurore* wool. The martingale is decorated with a heart-shaped brass plate, stamped with the traditional horn symbol of chasseurs.

Garde Impériale ~ Chasseurs à cheval. 1804-1815
Tenue de parade. 1804 - 1814.

PLATE 6

Garde Impériale – Chasseurs à cheval. 1804–1815
1805–1810. Trumpeter and *Brigadier-trompette*, parade uniform.

A decree of 29 July 1804 fixed the complement of the Chasseurs at four squadrons, each of two companies. Since there were three trumpeters to a company, the regiment had twenty-four trumpeters in all, led by a trumpet-major and two *brigadier-trompettes*. The addition of a fifth squadron, in 1811, increased the number of trumpeters to thirty, while the four squadrons of the Young Guard, created in 1813, had another twenty-four.

The trumpeters were part of the combat strength of the regiment. The most famous of them was Trumpet-major Elie Krettly, who won a *sabre d'honneur* at Mount Tabor and a *trompette d'honneur* at Marengo. At Austerlitz, he rescued his squadron commander from Russian grenadiers. In a second charge, leading his two platoons of trumpeters, he captured a Russian cannon. Eight of his men were awarded the Cross of the *Legion d'Honneur*. Krettly was promoted to *lieutenant en second*, then for similar actions at Eylau, to *porte-étendard d'honneur* and *lieutenant en premier*.

The braid, lace and cording of the trumpeter's dolman are woven in a third gold, two-thirds crimson, and a third gold, two-thirds sky-blue on his pelisse. As a *brigadier* trumpeter, his grade chevrons are of gold lace. The trim of his sabretache is of gold lace, and its coat of arms is on a blue ground. These splendid uniforms were reserved for special ceremonial parades. The crimson schabraques, with their borders of embroidered gold-linked chains and gold eagles, probably never left Paris. On campaign, they were replaced by sky-blue schabraques, trimmed with *aurore* bands, while the white trumpeters' colbacks were replaced by the black versions of the troopers.

Garde Impériale ~ Chasseurs à cheval. 1804.1815.

1805-1810. Trompette et Brigadier-trompette, tenue de parade.

PLATE 7

Garde Impériale – Chasseurs à cheval. 1804–1815
Maréchal-des-logis; *Maréchal-des-logis, trompette-major*; *Brigadier-trompette*.
In walking-out dress.

As the senior trumpeter of the regiment, the trumpet-major was a man of consequence. Here, he seems to have the respectful attention of his juniors. Beneath his gold-encrusted *habit* (dress coat), he wears a crimson waistcoat with five rows of fifteen buttons – later sixteen, and finally eighteen – criss-crossed with wool braid of a third gold and two-thirds sky-blue thread. His aiguillettes, however, are of mixed crimson and gold, in the same proportions. His Hungarian breeches are similarly decorated. His black felt hat, like that of his *brigadier-trompette*, is ornamented with four loops of gold braid and a wide lace loop, held in place over the cockade by a gilded button. *Marrons* (literally, chestnuts) of gold lace with crimson centres can be made out in the corners of his hat, which is topped with the same plume as the colback, mounted on flexible whalebone.

Except for the single chevron, the *brigadier-trompette*'s uniform is identical to that of his superior, but in his case we can see the gold-and-crimson trefoil worn on the right shoulder, and the embroidered chasseur's horn on a crimson backing, which decorates the *retroussis* (coat-tail linings) of his *habit*.

The dark green uniform of the *maréchal-des-logis* has the same grade distinctions, aiguillettes and ornamentation as the uniforms of his companions. In 1812, sword-knots of braided white wool with cord tassels replaced the white buff leather type previously used.

Garde Impériale ⚔ Chasseurs à cheval 1804-1815

Maréchal des logis ; Maréchal des logis, trompette-major ; Brigadier trompette. en tenue de ville.

PLATE 8

Garde Impériale – Chasseurs à cheval. 1804–1815
Trumpeters and chasseur. Dress walking-out uniform.

In this painting, we can see clearly the features that characterise the summer walking-out uniform of the Chasseur trumpeters. The gold lace on their collars and cuffs, and the crimson and blue braid of their breeches, waistcoats, aiguillettes and trefoils (each interwoven a third with gold thread), reflect their status as the equivalent of *sous-officiers*. Their boots, to which the spurs are screwed, are similarly trimmed. The gold *marrons* in the corners of their hats contrast with the simpler *aurore* version of their chasseur companion. The latter's waistcoat has three rows of buttons, while the more elaborate waistcoats of the trumpeters have five rows.

We may imagine what tale the trumpeter on the right is spinning for his comrades. Perhaps he is recalling the rainy night in October 1805, outside Ulm, when the Chasseurs requisitioned quarters reserved for the Emperor's carriages and wagons, then rudely ejected members of his civil household when they attempted to occupy their assigned billet. Aware that Napoleon referred to them as his *enfants chéris* (dear children), sometimes the Chasseurs stepped over the line, as they did on that occasion. Their punishment was to be deprived temporarily of the privilege of providing the Emperor's service squadron.

Writing of the *Chasseurs à cheval* of the Guard, Frédéric Masson said that there was not a battle at which Napoleon was present when the Chasseurs were not there, no *fête* to which they did not escort him. They were the troop that he kept for himself, of which he remained the master, a fact he proclaimed by always wearing their uniform when on campaign.

L. Rousselot

Garde Impériale - Chasseurs à cheval. 1804-1815

Trompettes et chasseur - Tenue de ville en habit.

PLATE 9

Garde Impériale – Chasseurs à cheval. 1804–1815
NCO, trumpeter and chasseur in Sunday walking-out dress. Winter.

These Chasseurs, dressed in their winter Sunday finery, are strolling past the café *Au Tambour d'Arcole*, apparently bent on some more agreeable diversion. The *sous-officier*'s dress differs from that of his comrades in several respects. His single gold lace chevron identifies him as a *maréchal-des-logis*, while the marmot fur trimming his pelisse is further evidence of his rank as a *sous-officier*. In common with the trumpeter, he has the mixed weaves of the braid on his pelisse, breeches and boots, while the ornamentation of the trooper's uniform is simple *aurore* braid.

Each wears his pelisse in the customary manner, with only the first few loops of braid on the left side of the garment slipped over the large buttons in the centre row of the jacket. The braided cord and toggle, which hold the pelisse on the trooper's left shoulder when it is worn in the hussar manner for parade dress, are neatly looped below the fur collar.

All three men are wearing their sabres, as prescribed by regulations for this dress, but not their showy sabretaches, which were only authorised for wear in town on Sundays between 1 May and 1 October.

Garde Impériale ~ Chasseurs à cheval 1804.1815

Sous-officier, trompette et chasseur en tenue de ville du Dimanche. (Hiver).

PLATE 10

Garde Impériale – Chasseurs à cheval. 1804–1815
Chasseur, trumpeter and officer, Sunday walking-out dress. Summer.

In this tranquil summer scene, a chasseur and his trumpeter comrade have interrupted their stroll through the park to refresh themselves with a *petit verre*. The chasseur insists that it is his turn to pay, reaching into his breeches pocket for a coin. In the background is a lieutenant of their regiment, who has found a pleasant companion.

This being a summer Sunday, the regulations prescribe the wearing of the sabretache with the sabre, thus enhancing appreciably the already striking uniforms of all three men. Their sabres, with blades forged by Coulaux *Frères* of Klingenthal, were designed specifically for the light cavalry of the Guard, being introduced into service in September 1803. The elegant, slightly curved form of the sabre became particularly associated with the Chasseurs of the Guard and continues to be evocative of that legendary corps.

Both chasseur and trumpeter are wearing their heavily braided dolmans, fastened only with loops of braid hooked over the top three large buttons in the centre of the garment. The trumpeter's service chevron is of gold lace, and the crimson lining of the lower portion of his dolman is visible as it hangs slightly open.

The dark green of the chasseur lieutenant's uniform is set off by his scarlet breeches, which have gold lace along their seams. The double rows of gold lace indicating his rank extend downward from his waist on to his thighs.

Garde Impériale – Chasseurs à cheval. 1804-1815.

Chasseur, trompette et officier, tenue de ville du dimanche. Eté.

PLATE 11

Garde Impériale – Chasseurs à cheval. 1804–1815
Officers and NCO in *redingotes*. Chasseur in stable dress.

Because the officers shown here are in their regimental depot on a weekday morning before ten o'clock, they are wearing their *redingotes* (light undress coats) and *bonnets de police* (fatigue caps). After that hour, their caps would be replaced by hats. The sabre of the officer in the background, whose ribbon of the *Légion d'Honneur* is sewn to his left breast, is suspended in a frog that emerges through a slit in his coat. In very cold weather, the officers would wear their *habits* or *surtouts* (undress coats) beneath their *redingotes*.

The *maréchal-des-logis*, noting his officer's orders for the day, is wearing his red morocco leather sword-belt. His aiguillettes, as well as the piping on his *bonnet de police*, its tassel and his sword-knot, are a combination of gold thread and crimson wool. His aiguillettes are worn on the left shoulder, while those of the officers are on their right shoulders, gold epaulettes being worn on the left.

The chasseur in stable dress wears a jacket with two rows of ten brass buttons. His duck trousers are fastened at each side by eighteen bone buttons. He wears the regulation *bonnet de police*. Guard officers were required to have servants and grooms. The latters' uniform comprised a green jacket with a yellow collar, and green or grey overalls. *Sous-officiers* and *trompettes* were allowed three grooms to a company. An order by Eugène de Beauharnais, commander of the regiment in 1803, required servants to wear a similar uniform, but this practice may not have extended to other regiments, or have been continued under later colonels.

Civilian servants, hired at the officers' personal expense, should not be confused with *ordonnances* (orderlies), who were soldiers of the regiment acting as 'batmen'.

L. Rousselot

Garde Impériale ~ Chasseurs à cheval 1804-1815

Officiers et sous-officier en redingote . Chasseur en tenue d'écurie .

PLATE 12

Garde Impériale – Chasseurs à cheval. 1804–1815
Officers. Walking-out and society dress. Chasseur in jacket.

Given the elegance of their surroundings, these officers may be in their regimental quarters in Paris. The officer on the left is being helped into his uniform *habit* by his *ordonnance*, but he has exchanged the scarlet or green Hungarian breeches of his service dress for breeches of fine cotton, linen or silk. His waistcoat is of similar fine material, lacking any decoration. Silk stockings and dress shoes with silver buckles complete his costume. He has removed the plume, excessively cumbersome for social occasions, from his hat.

His companion, who is evidently on duty this evening, is also in his *habit*, which is worn over his scarlet waistcoat with its five rows of buttons and courses of gold braid. Both officers are wearing their dress swords, or épées, suspended from white leather 'underneath' belts, which pass through the front flaps of their breeches. Black silk stocks around their necks add a touch of elegance to their appearance. The lieutenant on the right has the ribbon of the *Légion d'Honneur* attached to the lapel of his *habit* with a gold clasp.

The *ordonnance* is in his green stable jacket, worn with duck trousers. Orderlies were soldiers, who usually developed close and devoted relationships with the officers whom they served, and in whose company they fought on the battlefield.

Garde Impériale ~ Chasseurs à cheval. 1804.1815.

Officiers. Tenue de ville et tenue de société. Chasseur en veste.

PLATE 13

Garde Impériale – Chasseurs à cheval. 1804–1815
Maréchal-des-logis and troopers.

This *maréchal-des-logis* and his men are in full dress uniforms. The marmot fur trimming his pelisse, its green and gold braid, the gold rank and service chevrons on its sleeve, and the eagle embroidered in gold thread on his horse's schabraque, all serve to distinguish him from the troopers of the regiment. His sabre-tache, with its gold lace border, is of better quality than those of the troopers.

His single service chevron indicates ten years of service and means an extra franc a day in pay. Two chevrons would indicate fifteen years and one franc fifty extra; three chevrons would signify twenty years service and two extra francs per day.

The trooper on the right carries his carbine slung on the double cross-belt passing over his left shoulder, the other element of which bears his *giberne*. The carbine is the type issued to the corps in 1803 – actually the hussar musketoon of the 1786 model – fitted with a tenon to receive a bayonet, which is carried at the trooper's left side in a leather scabbard attached to his sword-belt.

The regiment's horses were bays and chestnuts, standing between 1.49 and 1.53 m at the withers – about fifteen hands. No doubt Rousselot's ability to depict horses with such fidelity is due, in some degree, to the fact that he served in the horse-drawn field artillery during the First and Second World Wars. In his studio were several exceptionally fine models of horses, which he had made as guides for his paintings.

Garde Impériale   Chasseurs à cheval 1804.1815.

Maréchal des logis et cavaliers.

PLATE 14

Garde Impériale – Chasseurs à cheval. 1804–1815
Field uniform. Austerlitz. 2 December 1805.

Here we see the Chasseurs in the pelisses that they wore during the campaign of 1805. The trumpeter, having sounded the charge, has slung his instrument on his back and taken up his sabre. He has pulled his schabraque back slightly to ensure that his pistols are ready for action in their holsters. The troopers' rolled cloaks are carried over their shoulders and across their chests for added protection.

At a critical point in the battle, when the Russian Guard cavalry was cutting up the 4th of the Line and had captured the first battalion's eagle, Napoleon instructed Marshal Bessières, commander of the Guard cavalry, 'Take two squadrons of my horse grenadiers and two of my chasseurs, and sweep those people away!' At Bessières' orders, Colonel Morland led forward two squadrons of Chasseurs, supported by three of Horse Grenadiers under General Ordener. The charge of the Chasseurs broke a square of the Semyenovski Guard regiment, which was screening the Russian Horse Guards, but the latter counter-attacked, driving the Chasseurs back and killing Morland.

Napoleon turned to his aide, General Rapp, saying, 'There's some confusion there. Go and put it right!' Rapp took the remaining Chasseur squadrons and the Mameluks, and swept down on the mêlée, driving off the Chevalier Guards and capturing Prince Repnin. However, carried ahead of his troops by the impetus of the charge, Rapp was wounded and had to be rescued by Mameluk Lieutenant Chaïm. Nevertheless, he was able to present his prisoners and captured flags to Napoleon. Finally, the tide was turned against the Russians when Bessières sent forward General Ordener with three squadrons of the Grenadiers.

Garde Impériale - Chasseurs à cheval. 1804-1815.

Tenue de charge - Austerlitz - 2 Décembre 1805.

PLATE 15

Garde Impériale – Chasseurs à cheval. 1804–1815
Officers in cloak and undress uniform.
This was the dress of the campaigns of 1806 and 1807.

The officers' voluminous cloaks, similar to those of the troopers, were designed to protect not only themselves, but also as much as possible of their horse furniture when mounted. The mounted lieutenant's 'little uniform' is none the less quite splendid, with its gold epaulette and aiguillettes, gold-trimmed *giberne banderole*, gold-braided waistcoat and officer's gold lace chevrons on the breeches.

Since the Treaty of Pressburg had been signed in the wake of Austerlitz, the Guard had spent much of 1806 in Paris, and it was late in the year before the start of the Prussian campaign. The Guard cavalry missed Jena/Auerstedt, and it was not until 8 February of the following year that the Chasseurs again took part in a major engagement, at Eylau in Poland. Fought in a blinding snowstorm, this ferocious combat cost both adversaries heavily.

Upon the death of Morland, Napoleon had given command of the Chasseurs to Major Dahlmann, as *colonel-commandant en seconde*. Then, in December Napoleon made Dahlmann a general, attaching him to his staff.

At the height of the battle, when Napoleon decided to employ the Chasseurs to support French infantry retreating under a Russian cavalry attack, Dahlmann asked for the honour of leading his old regiment, and Napoleon assented. Dahlmann led a charge of six Chasseur squadrons and the Mameluks, following on the heels of the Horse Grenadiers. Mortally wounded in the action, Dahlmann was brought back to the French lines, where he died the following day. The Chasseurs had lost twenty-one officers and 224 men killed or wounded that day.

Garde Impériale ~ Chasseurs à cheval 1804-1815.

Officiers en manteau et en petite tenue. Cette tenue fut celle des campagnes de 1806 et 1807.

PLATE 16

Garde Impériale – Chasseurs à cheval. 1804–1815
Escort dress. Campaigns of Prussia and Poland. 1806–1807.

This evidently being good weather, the chasseurs of the picket accompanying the Emperor are dressed in the *habits* of their service uniforms, the long ornamented tails of which fall down on each side of their saddles. The bayonet for the chasseur's carbine, slung on his right, is visible in the brown leather scabbard attached to his sword-belt.

The picket that accompanied Napoleon during his frequent excursions away from his field General Headquarters was drawn from the Chasseur service squadron and comprised a lieutenant, a *maréchal-des-logis*, two *brigadiers*, a trumpeter and twenty-two chasseurs, some riding in advance and some to the rear of the group immediately surrounding the Emperor. The latter included a *brigadier* and four chasseurs, one of whom carried Napoleon's portfolio containing his maps, writing materials and dividers, while another bore his telescope. Usually, Napoleon would be accompanied by his chief-of-staff, Marshal Berthier, the marshal on duty, several ADCs and orderly officers, the duty page, the Mameluk Roustam and possibly a surgeon if in a combat area.

Charles Parquin tells of an episode on such an occasion, which characterises the relationship between Napoleon and his *enfants chéris*. The horse of a chasseur riding ahead of the Emperor fell, throwing its rider. Riding past him, Napoleon called out that the trooper was a clumsy fellow. A few moments later, Napoleon himself took a tumble. The chasseur, having remounted, galloped past the fallen Master of Europe, remarking loudly enough for his voice to carry, 'It seems that I'm not the only clumsy fellow around here today!'

L. Rousselot

Garde Impériale ~ Chasseurs à cheval. 1804.1815.

Tenue d'escorte ~ Campagnes de Prusse et de Pologne 1806-1807

PLATE 17

Garde Impériale – Chasseurs à cheval. 1804–1815
March order. Campaigns of 1806 and 1807.

The most obvious distinguishing feature of the Chasseurs' uniforms worn during marches and on campaign were their dark green overalls, leather lined on the inside and around the bottoms, and closed on the outside by eighteen buttons sewn on scarlet lateral bands. The scarlet *flammes* of their colbacks have disappeared beneath black waxed and varnished silk covers atop the hats, and the plumes have been put away in black silk cases. The troopers' short queues are still tightly bound, but their hair is no longer powdered.

The muzzle of each trooper's carbine rests in a leather boot attached to his saddle, while a pommel strap, emerging from the saddle through the schabraque, restrains the butt-end of the weapon. The trooper's sabretache will be covered with a black, waxed and varnished case without ornament. The chasseur in the foreground has slung a gourd-like water bottle over his shoulder and hooked the points of his horse's schabraque up under his valise to prevent them from being soiled. Each man carries two bags of horse feed behind his saddle.

The *maréchal-des-logis* appears to be checking his men to ensure that their equipment is distributed correctly over their persons and mounts. The officer and the trumpeter observing the passing of the column in the distance are also in their *pantalons de voyage*, the trumpeter having exchanged his dress white fur colback for a standard Chasseur black colback.

Garde Impériale ~ Chasseurs à cheval 1804-1815

Tenue de route . Campagnes de 1806 et 1807.

PLATE 18

Garde Impériale – Chasseurs à cheval. 1804–1815
In Spain. 1808.

After a brief respite in Paris following the 1807 campaign, in early 1808 squadrons of the Chasseurs began to arrive in Spain. By that time, Napoleon's step-son and Viceroy in Italy, Eugène de Beauharnais, had given up his nominal command of the Chasseurs. In his place, they were commanded by *Général de brigade* Charles Lefèbvre-Desnouëttes.

A squadron under the command of Major Daumesnil, which had accompanied Murat to Madrid, was caught up in the insurrection that broke out there on 2 May. Ordered by Murat to aid French troops under attack, the Chasseurs had to fight their way through the centre of the city. There, Daumesnil had two horses shot from under him and had to be rescued by Mameluk Lieutenant Chaïm, who was wounded himself.

In pursuit of General Moore's army, in late December the Guard made a painful crossing of the Guadar-ramas in an icy snowstorm, the Chasseurs leading their horses on foot, with Napoleon in their midst. Five days later at Benavente, Lefèbvre-Desnouëttes led 500 Chasseurs and Mameluks in an attack on 600 British hussars and dragoons, and was captured during the action. Chasseur casualties were 165 killed, wounded or captured.

In 1808, the design of the Chasseurs' overalls was modified by eliminating the closures and buttons on the outside of each leg, the seams being covered by two stripes of *aurore* braid. By that time, the hunters' horns in the points of the schabraques had given way to Imperial eagles.

L. Rousselot

Garde Impériale ~ Chasseurs à cheval. 1804.1815

En Espagne. 1808.

PLATE 19

Garde Impériale – Chasseurs à cheval. 1804–1815
Campaign of 1809.

This chasseur and his trumpeter comrade have exchanged their travelling overalls and pelisses for breeches and dolmans, but are not dressed for escort service, since their colbacks do not display their corded and tasselled *flammes*, cockades or plumes. Perhaps they are crossing from the right bank of the Danube to the Isle of Lobau, where Napoleon was gathering his forces in anticipation of the Battle of Wagram, which took place on 6 July.

With Lefèbvre-Desnouëttes a British prisoner, Colonel Claude-Étienne Guyot took over the Chasseurs, together with all of the light cavalry, reporting to the Guard cavalry commander, General Count Walther. Daumesnil and Corbineau were Chasseur squadron commanders.

When Bessières, commanding the cavalry of the reserve, was wounded while charging at the head of the cuirassiers in an attack aimed between the corps of Lichtenstein and Kollowrath, Nansouty was left in command, but without orders from the Emperor. None the less, he continued the attack. When Napoleon saw that the Guard cavalry was hesitating, he ordered Walther to charge. As they did so, the Chasseurs broke through three of Kollowrath's squares. Daumesnil and Corbineau were wounded, the former losing a leg.

Walther ordered Guyot to launch the Chasseurs and the *Chevau-légers Polonais* in pursuit of the Austrians, who were withdrawing towards Gerarsdorf. When Guyot sighted four regiments of infantry and two of dragoons covering the Austrian retreat along the Brunn-Vienna road, he attacked and disrupted them, carrying off three cannon. Four officers and twenty chasseurs were killed.

Garde Impériale ~ Chasseurs à cheval. 1804-1815.

Campagne de 1809.

PLATE 20

Garde Impériale – Chasseurs à cheval. 1804–1815
Escort dress. 1812.

Whenever Napoleon came to a halt during his excursions in the field, the *brigadier* and the four chasseurs who rode directly ahead of him drew up also, forming a rough square around him, each facing outward. If the Emperor dismounted, they did also, fixing bayonets to their carbines, seen here hooked to the chasseur's cross-belt in readiness. The officer commanding the duty escort squadron had to remain within the sound of Napoleon's voice and be ready during that twenty-four-hour period to leap into his saddle at a moment's notice. Only Berthier and Murat had the privilege of inserting themselves between him and the Emperor.

The officer of the escort platoon was always in the room of the tent nearest to Napoleon's apartment. The other members of the picket were required to stand by the heads of their saddled and bridled horses, night and day, outside the entrance to the Imperial lodging. They were relieved every two hours. At all times, one of Napoleon's horses was held by two grooms in front of the picket's horses.

Notwithstanding these arrangements, on more than one occasion Napoleon thoughtlessly endangered himself, one notable incident occurring at Malojaroslavets, during the retreat from Moscow. Early in the day after that battle, wishing to visit the battlefield, Napoleon set out with a picket of Polish lancers, who mistook some cossacks for French cavalry. Recognising the danger, General Armand Caulaincourt, Duke of Vicenza, guided Napoleon's horse off the road, then led the service squadron in a charge on the cossacks. Bessières soon arrived on the scene with squadrons of Horse Grenadiers, Dragoons and Chasseurs, and drove off the cossacks. Nine Chasseurs were killed, and seven wounded.

L. Rousselot

Garde Impériale ~ Chasseurs à cheval. 1804-1815

Tenue d'escorte. 1812.

PLATE 21

Garde Impériale – Chasseurs à cheval. 1804–1815
Dress in cloaks.

These Chasseurs are wearing the combination cloak-overcoats with sleeves that were put into service in 1812. They have standing collars and are undecorated. In February 1804, small capes, the size of the upper elements of these cloaks, had been provided for the Chasseurs to wear over their cloaks during inclement weather, during service on foot, or when serving in Napoleon's mounted picket. The reason for wearing the small cape when on escort duty was because it permitted the distinctive Chasseur uniform to show, thus alerting others to the Emperor's presence.

For some time, there was a debate among uniform specialists as to whether both the large cloak and the cape had collars, or whether only one of them did, and, if so, which. Since no examples of either garment are known to have survived, the question remains unanswered.

It seems probable that the use of the cape as a separate element of uniform did not survive after 1807, if only because it failed to protect the Chasseur's thighs and equipage, unlike the large cloaks shown in this painting.

The artist has given his Chasseur the side-buttoned overalls which, he tells us in the text for his *planches*, had been replaced in 1808 by overalls with side seams covered by a double *aurore* band. Given Rousselot's rigorous attention to detail, it seems likely that he learned the date of the change in overall design after he had painted this picture.

L. Rousselot

Garde Impériale ～ Chasseurs à cheval. 1804 1815.

Tenue en manteau.

PLATE 22

Garde Impériale – Chasseurs à cheval. 1804–1815
Officer, troopers and trumpeter, campaign dress. 1812.

This captain's campaign dress includes his dolman, his overalls with gold lace stripes, his braided cord sash and his colback, which is bare of ornamentation, save for its cockade. His undress sabretache is decorated with a gilded bronze Imperial coat of arms and framed with a gilded fillet. The elaborate and expensive *banderole* carrying his *giberne* is protected by a buttoned morocco leather covering, and he is wearing his undress sabre.

By 1811, the Chasseurs' overalls had been redesigned, their leather reinforcements being replaced by an extra layer of green cloth, and their side seams closed and covered by double *aurore* stripes. The sabretaches worn here are in black waxed cloth cases, decorated with painted Imperial eagles. The trumpeter's white colback is surprising, since Rousselot says that the dress colbacks were left at the regiment's depot, black colbacks always being worn on campaign.

General Lefèbvre-Desnouëttes had returned from England in 1811, in violation of his parole, and in May 1812, he resumed his position as commander of the Chasseurs. During the Russian campaign, he led a division of the Old Guard cavalry as well. Although the Chasseurs, and the Guard as a whole, were not called upon to participate in the major battles of the Russian campaign (Smolensk and Borodino), the constant skirmishing and the extreme weather during the retreat took a heavy toll on the regiment. It lost some 500 men from the five Old Guard squadrons and the company of Mameluks with which it had begun the campaign.

Garde Impériale ~ Chasseurs à cheval 1804-1815.

Officier, cavaliers et trompette, tenue de campagne. 1812.

PLATE 23

Garde Impériale – Chasseurs à cheval. 1804–1815
Young Guard squadrons. Full dress. 1813.

Many elements of the uniforms of the Chasseurs of the four newly-formed Young Guard squadrons were identical to those of the Old Guard Chasseurs: the dolmans, breeches, corded sashes, overalls, cloaks, *bonnets de police* and stable dress. They were made of poorer quality materials, however, and their buff leather belts were not stitched along the edges in the style of the Old Guard.

That said, there were striking differences. The most obvious of these was the scarlet schako, trimmed with *aurore* braid and cords, and decorated in the front with a brass eagle and cockade. These were surmounted by the standard Chasseur red-on-green plume, at the base of which was a red pompom.

Other instantly recognisable differences were the Young Guard Chasseurs' scarlet portmanteaus and schabraques, both trimmed with green tape. The seats of the schabraques were covered with white sheep-skin, and their points were without any decoration. The Young Guards' sabretaches were simply of black leather. Here, Rousselot has ornamented them with brass eagles, although in the text for his *Planche* No. 70 (published in 1960, after he had made this painting), he speculates that the decoration may have been the arms of the Empire.

Instructors, *brigadiers* and NCOs of these squadrons were principally drawn from Old Guard squadrons, and they continued to wear the uniforms of the Old Guard. They used the same horse furniture as their Young Guard troopers, however.

L. Rousselot

Garde Impériale ~ Chasseurs à cheval. 1804-1815.

Escadrons de Jeune Garde - Grande tenue - 1813.

Plate 24

Garde Impériale – Chasseurs à cheval. 1804–1815
Young Guard squadrons. Campaign dress. 1813.

Troopers of the Young Guard squadrons were young men who had been offered to Napoleon by cities, corporations and departments. They had been chosen for their height, physical qualities and ability to ride. They were referred to as *seconds chasseurs*, in contrast to the *premiers chasseurs* of the Old Guard squadrons. Their officers came from the Old Guard, however, and were required to have had twelve years of Guard service, four in grade.

The *seconds chasseurs* in this painting have stowed their plumes and schako cords, and have wound their cloaks over their shoulders and across their chests for protection. They are wearing the overalls with double *aurore* stripes introduced in 1808, although these trousers have leather inserts, in contrast to those of the Old Guard Chasseurs. Under the circumstances prevailing in 1813 France, it is hardly surprising that there were inconsistencies in the supply of uniforms for new formations.

Général de division Lefèbvre-Desnouëttes was still *Colonel en premier* of the corps, with *Général de division* Guyot as his *Colonel en second*. The Old Guard squadrons were under the command of *Colonel-major* Lion, while *Colonel-major* Meuziau commanded the Young Guard squadrons. By December of that year, the Young Guard squadrons were referring to themselves as the *Deuxième Régiment de Chasseurs à cheval de la Jeune Garde*, but that designation was not official.

L. Rousselot

Garde Impériale ∝ Chasseurs à cheval. 1804-1815.

Escadrons de Jeune Garde. Tenue de campagne. 1813.

PLATE 25

Garde Impériale – Chasseurs à cheval. 1804–1815
Young Guard squadrons. Trumpeter. 1813–1814.

At first glance, it is surprising to see this Young Guard trumpeter in a colback and pelisse, neither of which were issued to the Chasseurs of these squadrons. However, it will be recalled that the cadres for these newly formed squadrons were men from Old Guard squadrons. This trumpeter, then, is one of that group. Consequently, he has brought with him his black campaign colback and his crimson pelisse, with its mingled gold and sky-blue braiding. His sword-knot is the Old Guard version comprising two braided cords, unlike the white buff leather type issued to the Young Guard. The apparent absence of an eagle on his sabretache suggests that he has drawn a black oiled silk cover over it.

Fashions in overalls seem to have changed frequently. This trumpeter's overalls are of 'Marengo' grey cloth with leather reinforcing between the legs and around the bottoms, and a double crimson stripe along each outside seam.

The officer in the background on the right is another member of the Old Guard cadre, but both his and the trumpeter's mounts are carrying Young Guard horse furniture.

The Chasseurs in the skirmish line are wearing the new tall, cylindrical schako, which replaced the more familiar 'classic' colback of the Napoleonic era, with its outward tapering form. The schakos' brilliant scarlet is concealed beneath black waxed cloth protective coverings, topped by their pompoms.

I. Rousselot

Garde Impériale ~ Chasseurs à cheval. 1804-1815.

Escadrons de Jeune Garde   Trompette 1813-1814.

PLATE 26

Garde Impériale – Chasseurs à cheval. 1804–1815
Young Guard squadrons. Campaign dress. 1814.

In December 1813, Napoleon confirmed the *de facto* division of the Chasseurs into two regiments by sending all but one company of the Young Guard squadrons, under *Colonel-major* Meuziau, north to Belgium to join General Maison's *Armée d'Anvers*. Remaining with the Old Guard squadrons, as part of the much reduced *Grande Armée*, was the 11th company of the 6th squadron of the Young Guard Chasseurs, under Captain Charles Parquin. On 3 January 1814, the Old Guard regiment, commanded by *Général-major* Lion, left Paris for Rheims. By this time, the five Old Guard squadrons had been reduced to a strength of forty officers and 638 men.

Let us assume that when he painted this picture, the artist had in mind Parquin's Young Guard company, marching and fighting almost constantly over several months alongside their Old Guard mentors. He has depicted Young Guard Chasseurs clashing with Russian cuirassiers, perhaps at Brienne on 29 January, when Lefèbvre-Desnouëttes was wounded and thrown from his horse while leading a charge of the Chasseurs and Horse Grenadiers. Less battle-hardened though they were, the Young Guard Chasseurs fought as valiantly and successfully as their veteran comrades.

Here, we can clearly see the new schakos issued to the Young Guard squadrons, notable for their fully cylindrical form, their scarlet cloth covering and their turned-up black leather neck-shields. The only decorations are a cockade, held in place by a strap of gold braid, and a pompom.

Garde Impériale ~ Chasseurs à cheval. 1804-1815.

Escadrons de Jeune Garde . Tenue de Campagne . 1814.

PLATE 27

Garde Impériale – Chasseurs à cheval. 1804–1815
Campaign of France. 1814.

In the course of the three-month Campaign of France, which began in mid-January and led to the fall of Paris, the Guard cavalry participated in fifteen battles, as well as almost daily lesser skirmishes, forming the indispensable core of Napoleon's steadily shrinking army. In almost every instance, facing enemy forces many times their own strength, these indomitable men launched charges on Russian, Prussian and Austrian formations with the same reckless courage, determination and selflessness that they had demonstrated in the most glorious days of the Empire.

In this painting, Rousselot has portrayed vividly the calm and fearless determination with which the Guard Chasseurs and their comrades successfully pressed home their charges, often under seemingly impossible circumstances. Marching and counter-marching across eastern France almost continuously between engagements, often in atrocious weather conditions and with few opportunities to eat and rest, their dedication to the Emperor and their willingness to obey his every order without question never wavered.

Extraordinary feats of arms became almost commonplace in the Guard cavalry. Reporting to Napoleon on the Battle of Saint-Dizier on 26 March, after he had driven off Wintzingerode's forces with the Guard cavalry, General Sébastiani stated, 'I have served twenty years as a cavalry officer, and I cannot recall ever seeing a more brilliant charge than that of the leading squadron today.' He was referring to the Chasseurs of Major Kirmann, including Captain Parquin and his Young Guard company.

Garde Impériale ~ Chasseurs à cheval. 1804-1815.

Campagne de France . 1814.

PLATE 28

Garde Impériale – Chasseurs à cheval. 1804–1815
Campaign dress. 1815.

Here, we see evidence of the strain of re-establishing and re-equipping the Imperial Guard during the One Hundred Days. The troopers' old-style, side-buttoned overalls have been resurrected from the Corps' depot stores, while undress schabraques, minus their Imperial eagles, form the horse housings. If the plumes, cockades and cords of the colbacks have been located and issued, they are stowed in portmanteaus.

The Guard had been re-established by a decree of 21 March, and another, of 8 April, had set the composition of each Guard cavalry regiment at four squadrons. Lefèbvre-Desnouëttes was given command of the light cavalry division, with General François-Antoine Lallemand commanding the Chasseurs, and General Edouard Colbert, the Lancers. On the 15th, Napoleon said to Ney, 'I give you also the light cavalry of the Guard – but don't use it!' A rather ambiguous command!

On 18 June, the Guard cavalry had been placed in the third line, with Reille's 2nd Corps in the first line, and Kellermann's cavalry in the second. Ney had stationed Lefèbvre-Desnouëttes' light cavalry in reserve, behind the cuirassiers. There are several versions as to what occurred at the turning point of the battle. One has it that Ney suddenly appeared in front of the Chasseurs and Lancers, calling out, 'Frenchmen, the keys of your liberty are here! We must save the Empire, we must save France! Follow me!'

The mass of cavalry followed him up the slope to the waiting British squares, against which they repeatedly dashed themselves, but to no avail. Lefèbvre-Desnouëttes, Lallemand and Colbert were wounded, and the Guard cavalry lost 1700 men that day.

L. Rousselot

Garde Impériale ~ Chasseurs à cheval. 1804-1815.

Tenue de campagne. 1815.

PLATE 29

Garde Impériale – Grenadiers à cheval. 1805–1809
Brigadier-trompette, trumpeters and kettledrummer. Parade uniform.

The bright, glittering uniforms worn by these soldiers and the splendour of their mounts' equipage reflected the extraordinary esteem enjoyed by this prestigious regiment. As the *tête de colonne* in a parade, the *timbalier* and trumpeters contrasted sharply with the relatively sombre uniforms of the towering *Grenadiers à cheval* who followed them. The latters' dress closely resembled that of their infantry counterparts.

Regiments vied with one another in dressing their *timbaliers* in spectacular fashion, but few could have equalled the brilliance of the hussar-style costume worn by this young kettledrummer, or his gold-laced and tasselled drum banners and schabraque. No doubt his visorless crimson schako, criss-crossed with bands of gold lace, was one of a kind. In 1811, the *timbalier* received a dolman of scarlet cloth with a blue collar and cuffs, decorated with gold frogging and trim. However, further details of that uniform are lacking.

These splendid uniforms were reserved for occasions of great importance. There were only slight modifications to the trumpeters' parade dress during the entire period of the Empire. For example, in 1806, shoulder trefoils were replaced by the counter-epaulettes shown in this painting. In 1809, the composition of the aiguillettes was changed from a third gold thread and two-thirds crimson wool to two-thirds gold, a third wool. At the same time, undress aiguillettes with only a seventh gold admixture were provided.

Garde Impériale. Grenadiers à cheval. 1805-1809.
Brigadier-trompette, trompettes et timbalier
Tenue de parade.

PLATE 30

Garde Impériale – Grenadiers à cheval. 1805–1813
Trumpeters in undress uniforms. 1. Walking-out in undress coat – summer – 1805–1809.
2. Campaign uniform in undress *habit*, 1809–1812.
3. In three-quarters cloak, 1805–1813. 4. Campaign full dress, 1806–1808.

In his walking-out dress, the trumpeter on the left wears nankeen breeches and his undress hat. His aiguillettes are the undress version, and his sword-belt is worn over his shoulder *en baudrier*.

The undress *habit* worn by his mounted comrade differs in two respects from Rousselot's depiction in *Planche* No. 45 of the undress *habit* in use at this time: the buttonholes of its *revers* lack gold lace tabs; and the cuff flaps are sky-blue, rather than crimson. (Perhaps it is a *second habit*.) The belt buckles of both trumpeters are stamped with grenades, whereas Rousselot's research – presumably completed after this painting was finished – indicated that in 1808 the stamping was changed to a crowned eagle. The rider's bearskin has been stripped of its cording and plume, and he is wearing side-buttoned duck overalls over his deerskin breeches.

The 'three-quarters' cloak worn by the trumpeter in the background is of the sleeveless type, which continued in use until at least 1813, and possibly 1814. When the cloaks were folded for strapping on to the portmanteaus, the crimson serge lining was displayed. Neither portmanteau nor cloak was worn with the dress housings, however.

Since no lapels are visible on the coat of the dismounted trumpeter, in what is identified as campaign full dress, he would appear to be wearing a *surtout*, rather than a *habit*, which would seem appropriate for campaign full dress. He has dressed his bearskin cap with its cords and plume. His boots are the type with stiff tops and flexible legs.

L. Rousselot

Garde Impériale. Grenadiers à cheval. 1805-1813

Trompettes en petit uniforme. 1 tenue de ville en surtout - été - 1805-1809. 2. tenue de campagne

en habit de petit uniforme 1809-1812. 3 En manteau trois-quarts 1805-1813. 4. Grande tenue de campagne 1806-1808

PLATE 31

Garde Impériale – Grenadiers à cheval. 1804–1814
Walking-out dress. 1. In undress coat, 1804–1808. 2. In 'second' dress coat, 1808–1814.
3. Sunday dress in summer, 1804–1808. 4. Same dress, 1808–1814.

Both Grenadiers on the left are in undress uniforms. The *surtout* worn by No. 1 was replaced in 1809 by the undress *habit* worn by No. 2. The latter was of less expensive material than that used for the dress *habit*, and differed from it in having plain round cuffs, rather than round scarlet cuffs with white slashes. Both men wear their deerskin breeches, white cloth sleeves protecting the latter from the rubbing of their soft boots *à l'écuyère*. No. 1's hat is decorated with *aurore* wool loops, which were eliminated after 1811.

The Sunday summer walking-out dress of the Grenadiers on the right requires them to appear in their dress *habits*, nankeen breeches buckled at the knees, and in silk stockings and silver-buckled shoes. Both have powdered coiffeurs, the little silver grenade that decorated all queue black ribbons being visible on No. 3. The *brigadier* wears two service chevrons on his sleeve, while his companion has earned one, as well as the Star of the Legion. (Three hundred Horse Grenadiers were awarded the Star.)

The scabbard of No. 3's sabre is the reinforced version with two 'windows', which replaced a weaker scabbard that required two strengthening bracelets. All four Grenadiers wear their sword-belts over the right shoulder *en baudrier*. The preferred mode of wearing the *chapeau* seems to be cocked over the right eye.

L. Rousselot

Garde Impériale — Grenadiers à cheval. 1804-1814.

Tenues de ville. — 1. en surtout, 1804-1808. — 2. en second habit, 1808-1814.

— 3. tenue du dimanche en été, 1804-1808. — 4. même tenue, 1808-1814.

PLATE 32

Garde Impériale – Grenadiers à cheval. 1808–1812
Eagle-bearer lieutenant escorted by two NCOs and three *brigadiers.*

Selection as a *porte-aigle* was usually a reward for a notable act of bravery, as in the case of Elie Krettly of the Chasseurs of the Guard, who was promoted to *lieutenant en premier* and *porte-aigle* for his actions at Eylau. The eagle of the Horse Grenadiers' standard has around its neck the gold wreath awarded to regiments returning to Paris after Austerlitz. A grenade, rather than a regimental number, decorates its base. The standard itself is the 1804 model, which was carried by the regiment throughout the Russian campaign.

The officer and his *maréchaux-des-logis* escorts are wearing their Stars of the Legion. His white plume indicates his status as a member of the regimental staff. He is wearing his dress sabre, with its guard *à la grenade*, a hallmark of the Grenadiers' sabres. The cords and flounders of the *sous-officiers'* bearskin caps and their aiguillettes are of mixed crimson wool and gold thread. All wear their stiff dress boots.

The dress saddle-cloths of all the Grenadiers are of the type introduced in 1808, Imperial crowns replacing grenades in their corners. (Undress saddle-cloths retained their grenades.) At the same time, black rubbing leathers were added to the sides of the saddle-cloths. For dress parades, the horses' harness included white surcingles, their forelocks being braided with red ribbon and attached to the near-side of their headstalls under red cockades. Larger cockades were attached to their crupper-loops. Here, the *sous-officiers'* blue cloaks are strapped behind the cantles of their saddles, while their portmanteaus have been left at the barracks.

Garde Impériale Grenadiers à cheval 1808-1812

Lieutenant porte-aigle escorté de deux sous-officiers
et de trois brigadiers

PLATE 33

Garde Impériale – Grenadiers à cheval. 1805–1814
Senior officer. Mounted full dress 1809–1814. Junior officers.
Walking-out in dress or undress coat.

In this painting, the height of the mounted officer's bearskin cap is particularly noticeable. The Year X regulations prescribed a height of 31.8 cm (about 12.5 in) for such headgear, but the reality seems to have been closer to 35.0 cm (about 13.75 in). This officer's *bonnet* may even exceed that height; compare it to the *bonnet* worn by the *porte-aigle* in the previous painting. Together with the triple-layered, heavily gold-laced hoods covering his pistol holsters, it is an attribute of his senior rank. He is wearing the Star of the Legion, and his dress sabre is suspended at his side.

Of the two officers in their walking-out dress, the round, blue cuffs of his coat indicate that the one on the left is in his *surtout*, while his companion wears his *habit*. The latter's left *revers* (lapel) is decorated with the ribbon of his Cross, and his white collar emerges from that of his coat. In the first design of both *surtouts* and *habits*, their *retroussis* had been free-floating and hooked together. In a second design, the *retroussis* were sewn to the body of the garment, leaving visible beneath their joined points a small blue triangle of cloth. Finally, towards 1811, the triangle disappeared, as can be seen on the coats of all three officers. Both pleasure-bent officers have put aside their sabres for their dress épées.

In the background are grenadiers, whose white cloaks are strapped to the tops of their portmanteaus behind the cantles of their saddles, their partial scarlet linings being displayed.

Garde Impériale – Grenadiers à cheval 1805-1814
Officier supérieur. Grande tenue à cheval 1809-1814.
Officiers subalternes. Tenue de ville en habit ou en surtout.

L. Rousselot

PLATE 34

Garde Impériale – Grenadiers à cheval. 1809–1814
Trumpet-major in parade uniform, and trumpeter in stable dress.

From his expression, this trumpet-major seems well aware of the splendour of his appearance in his parade uniform, seated as he is in his crimson and gold-laced saddle housing, astride his dappled white horse. Who could blame him? He is lofty dignity personified. The trumpeter, in his stable jacket, *bonnet de police* and side-buttoning duck trousers, respectfully awaits the command to proffer his superior's gleaming trumpet.

In Plate 29, the obverse side of the trumpet banner, bearing a crowned 'N', can be seen. The reverse side shown here displays an eagle with spread wings, the same design as used on the reverse of the regimental standard. (In his *Planche* No. 45, Rousselot places a grenade in each corner of the banner.)

The trumpet-major's full dress *chapeau* is one of thirty bought for the regiment in 1809, and described as being of the same quality as those issued to general officers. The gold lace loops of the earlier model have been discarded, and into its broad gold lace border are woven crowns and grenades. The seams of the sleeves and the back of the trumpet-major's dress *habit* are covered with gold lace. In this painting, the artist has added sky-blue slashes to his round cuffs, while in *Planche* No. 45 they are shown as crimson.

His horse's snaffle-bridle is of woven yellow-gold thread, while the gilded boss of the harness bit is decorated with a grenade in relief.

I. Rousselot

Garde Impériale - Grenadiers à cheval - 1809-1814.

Trompette-major en tenue de parade.

et trompette en tenue d'écurie.

PLATE 35

Garde Impériale – Grenadiers à cheval. 1809–1814
Brigadier, troopers, officer and trumpeter. Service dress.

The service dress of these Grenadiers would be worn, for example, when their squadron was assigned to the immediate service of the Emperor. It is identical to their parade uniforms, including even the horses' braided forelocks and crupper rosettes. The trumpeter, however, wears his undress *habit*. In addition to the absence of gold-laced buttonholes on his coat's *revers*, the plume on his bearskin is sky-blue, rather than crimson and white, as depicted in *Planche* No. 45.

While a Chasseur's equipment included a carbine sling as a means of keeping his weapon readily available for use, the greater length of the musket issued to Grenadiers made a sling impractical. Thus the stock of the musket was seated in a boot attached to the saddle, and its barrel restrained by a strap attached to the pommel. Whether the Horse Grenadiers had occasion to use their muskets in combat is difficult to ascertain, yet their potential employment must have been an important justification for imposing this substantial burden on horse and rider.

The artist's love of horses is especially evident in his depiction of the glistening animal in the foreground of this painting. The Grenadiers' powerful black horses were an important element in their image, but in the waning days of the Empire, especially after the enormous losses of horses during the Russian campaign, it became impossible to maintain consistency in the coats of the Grenadiers' mounts.

L. Rousselot

Garde Impériale. Grenadiers à cheval. 1809-1814.

Brigadier, cavaliers, officier et trompette.

Tenue de service.

PLATE 36

Garde Impériale – Grenadiers à cheval. 1804–1814
Officer in undress. NCO in *redingote*. Grenadier in stable dress.
Grenadier in Sunday walking-out dress.

We can date this scene to before 1811, because it was in that year that the loops – gold lace in the case of the officer, and *aurore* on the grenadier's *chapeau* – disappeared. We can push it back another two years, because the stable jackets worn by the grenadiers are fitted with thirteen brass buttons, an arrangement that was modified in 1809 to provide fifteen buttons. It is also no earlier than 1806, because it was probably then that the shoulder trefoils of the Grenadiers were replaced by the *contre-epaulettes* seen on the *maréchal-des-logis-chef* and the grenadier.

The officer and *sous-officier* are wearing their 'soft' boots *à l'écuyère*, customary for service on foot or 'in town', and their sabres have been replaced by their dress épées. On the officer's breast is the ribbon of an officer of the Legion. The *maréchal-des-logis-chef*'s aiguilettes, his sword-knot, and the piping and tassel of his *bonnet de police* are all of mixed gold thread and scarlet wool.

We also know that the scene takes place on a Sunday, because the grenadier in his walking-out dress has donned his nankeen breeches, silk stockings and silver-buckled shoes, while he has hung his sword-belt over his right shoulder *en baudrier*. Rousselot has placed *aurore* tufts in the corners of the grenadier's *chapeau*, whereas in his *Planche* No. 23, the artist shows these *marrons* as scarlet.

Garde Impériale - Grenadiers à cheval. 1804-1814.

Officier en petite tenue. Sous-officier en redingote.

Grenadier en tenue d'écurie. Grenadier en tenue de ville du dimanche.

PLATE 37

Garde Impériale – Grenadiers à cheval. 1805–1814
Officers. Campaign uniforms: in undress coat from 1805 to 1808; in three-quarters cloak;
in dress coat from 1809 to 1814.

General Lepic, who was deputy commander of the Horse Grenadiers on 8 February 1807 at Eylau, is perhaps best remembered for his shouted exhortation to his troops, some of whom were bending over their horses' necks under a hail of Russian fire, *'Haut les têtes, Jarnidiou! Ce sont des boulets, pas de la merde!'* ('Heads up, Goddammit! Those are bullets, not turds!'). However, he deserves more to be remembered for an extraordinary action at a later stage of the battle.

When Murat and the reserve cavalry charged and became trapped behind Russian forces, Napoleon ordered Bessières to free them with the Guard cavalry. Bessières launched the Chasseurs, the Grenadiers and the Mameluks against the Russian lines. At the head of the Grenadiers, Lepic and his men broke through the first and second lines, then dispersed several support battalions, the general finally reaching open ground with some thirty of the Grenadiers around him. A squadron of Russian dragoons rapidly encircled them, and their officer called to Lepic in French, 'Surrender, General! Your courage has carried you too far – you are in our lines.'

Gesturing at his men with his sabre, Lepic replied, 'Look at those mugs and tell me if they want to surrender! Grenadiers, follow me!' With that, he and his men spurred back through the dragoons and Russian lines.

When Napoleon saw Lepic, he joyfully greeted him, saying, 'I thought you had been made a prisoner, General, and I was deeply pained!' Lepic replied, 'Sire, you will never hear but of my death!'

The officer at the left in this painting, with his ribbon of the Legion and his clubbed hair style, might well have been one of those Grenadiers, who received the Star and a battlefield promotion for that day's work.

Garde Impériale ~ Grenadiers à cheval. 1805-1814.

Officiers. Tenues de campagne : en surtout de 1805 à 1808 ;

en manteau trois-quarts ; en habit de 1809 à 1814.

PLATE 38

Garde Impériale – Grenadiers à cheval. 1806–1814
Campaign uniforms. 1. In undress coat, 1806–1807. 2. In undress coat, 1807–1809.
3. In undress *habit*, 1810–1814.

The *surtout* worn by No. 2 in this painting differs from No. 1's in that it is cut lower in front and fastened with ten buttons, rather than the six or seven of the earlier model. All three Grenadiers have side-buttoned overalls of drill over their deerskin or sheep's-hide breeches to protect them. (Perhaps those are their dress breeches tucked under the flaps of their portmanteaus.)

In 1809, the undress *habit* worn by No. 3 replaced the *surtout* for the troopers of the regiment, although the *surtout* continued to be issued to *brigadiers* and *sous-officiers* until 1814. It differs from the dress version in that it is of poorer quality material and has the round blue cuffs of the *surtout*, rather than the scarlet cuffs with white slashes of the dress *habit*.

The scabbard of No. 1's sabre *à la Montmorency* is the first type issued to the regiment. This had an inherent weakness that necessitated reinforcement with two bracelets over the single long openings in each side of its brass sheath. (This task might well have been accomplished by the regiment's armourers, who were trained at the factory in Versailles.) It was only in 1810 that the factory produced a stronger model with two separate 'windows' on each side, with which No. 3 is equipped.

The painting clearly illustrates the stitching along the edges of the Grenadiers' cross- and waist-belts, a distinction peculiar to the Guard.

The picket posted on the rise in the background seems to have found a practical use for his musket.

L. Rousselot

Garde Impériale . Grenadiers à cheval. 1806-1814.

Tenues de campagne : 1 en surtout 1806-1807, 2 en surtout 1807-1809.

3 en habit de petit uniforme 1810-1814.

PLATE 39

Garde Impériale – Grenadiers à cheval. 1813.
NCO, grenadier and trumpeter in three-quarters cloaks (in use until 1813). Grenadier in caped overcoat, 1813–1815, identical for NCOs, trimmed in crimson for trumpeters.

The shabby, weather-stained attire of these chilled, but resolute, Grenadiers, glimpsed probably in late October in the aftermath of the French defeat in the 'Battle of the Nations' at Leipzig, may call to mind the words that Shakespeare attributed to an earlier monarch:

We are but warriors for the working day;
Our gayness and our gilt are all beschmirch'd
With rainy marching in the painful field;
But, by the mass, our hearts are in the trim.

The gleaming sabres and steadfast countenances of these soldiers reflect the undaunted spirit that continued to sustain the Imperial Guard, in the face of all its adversities, as the most respected – and feared – military formation in the world at that time.

During the inconclusive French victories at Lützen, Bautzen and, after the summer's armistice had been broken, Dresden, the Guard cavalry was not heavily engaged. Nor was it called upon to play a decisive role at Leipzig. Its commander, Marshal Bessières, had been killed on the eve of Lützen by a stray cannon-ball and replaced by Nansouty.

Finally, at Hanau on 30 October, the tattered remnants of the *Grande Armée* slashed their way through the blockade of von Wrede's Bavarians, opening the road back to France.

Garde Impériale - Grenadiers à cheval. 1813.

Sous officier, grenadier et trompette en manteau trois quarts (en usage jusqu'en 1813.)

Grenadier en manteau capote 1813-1815. identique pour sous-officiers, garni en cramoisi pour trompettes

PLATE 40

Garde Impériale – Grenadiers à cheval. 1804–1815
Troopers of the Young Guard squadrons, 1813–1814.

In January 1813, the four Old Guard squadrons of the regiment were augmented by two Young Guard squadrons, made up of men who had been offered to Napoleon by the towns and departments near Paris. They were referred to as *seconds grenadiers* or *cavaliers seconds*, given the pay of Line regiments and were not – as we see in this painting – authorised to wear aiguillettes. In addition, they did not wear the Old Guard's powdered and clubbed coiffures or golden ear-rings, and their buff leather equipment lacked the distinctive Guard stitching along its edges.

By 1813, the grey trousers worn by these *seconds grenadiers* had been introduced for the Guard cavalry. They were reinforced between the legs and on the outside of the thighs to reduce wear from the friction of sabres and muskets. These troopers wear the undress *habit*, with the plain round cuffs of the *surtout*. Their horses' saddle-cloths are of the undress model, which retained the grenade decoration, rather than crowns.

The Grenadiers of the Young Guard squadrons were led by Old Guard officers. During the German campaign of 1813, inspired by their own enthusiasm and the reputation and example of their 'elders', they met with the Emperor's approbation whenever they were engaged.

The Campaign of France in the following year saw the Guard, now making up a third of the *Grande Armée*, engaged in an almost constant series of skirmishes and pitched battles, and marches and counter-marches, continually suffering irreplaceable losses. As the end drew near, Napoleon lamented that 'the Young Guard cavalry melted like snow.' As indeed it did.

Garde Impériale – Grenadiers à cheval. 1804.1815.

Cavaliers des escadrons de Jeune-Garde. 1813-1814.

PLATE 41

Garde Impériale – Grenadiers à cheval. 1815
The regiment, which had become the Royal Corps of Cuirassiers of France in 1814,
had not yet received its armour in 1815, but was already wearing the *habit-veste* with
which it fought the Campaign of Belgium.

The sky in this painting, intentionally or not, suggests the blazing pyre of 'The Twilight of the Gods'. After all, were not the Horse Grenadiers of the Guard sometimes referred to as 'the gods'? These men were warriors, not Valkyries, but they were to be plunged into the fire of the battlefield at Waterloo.

In their role as the Royal Corps of Cuirassiers of France, the Grenadiers had been given the *habit-vestes* worn by those cavalrymen in anticipation of their receiving cuirasses. These coats were piped in red along the front opening, but lacked the long tails and the white *revers* of the old *habits*, their only ornamentation being red cuffs with white three-button slashes. Perhaps there had been time before Waterloo to replace the buttons bearing the fleur-de-lis with others displaying the Imperial eagle. Rather than accepting steel helmets to accompany the cuirasses, the regiment had managed to retain its distinctive bearskins.

In early May, 243 troopers of the former Young Guard squadrons had asked to rejoin their old comrades, and had been welcomed into the regiment's four squadrons. On the field of Waterloo on 18 June, the Grenadiers participated in the premature and fruitless massed cavalry attacks upon the British squares on Mont Saint Jean. At eight that evening, the service squadrons made the final charge of the Guard cavalry, in an effort to prevent the French from being driven from the field. When that attack failed, the Horse Grenadiers withdrew at a walk, and in good order. All was lost, save honour.

J. Rousselot

Garde Impériale - Grenadiers à cheval 1815.

Le régiment devenu Corps Royal des Cuirassiers de France en 1814, n'avait pas encore reçu

ses armures en 1815, mais il portait déjà l'habit-veste avec lequel il fit la campagne de Belgique.

PLATE 42

Garde Impériale – Dragons de l'Impératrice. 1806–1815
Officer. Parade uniform. 1806–1808.

The Dragoons were established by the Emperor's decree of 15 April 1806. On 19 May, Napoleon appointed as the regiment's commander a second cousin, Colonel Jean-Toussaint Arrighi de Casanova, giving him the Guard rank of major-colonel and the responsibility for designing the regiment's uniforms. Arrighi adopted the basic design of the Horse Grenadiers' uniform, changing its blue colour to the traditional dark green associated with dragoons. Wishing to create a 'modern' uniform, he did away with queues, powdered hair and other such 'accessories'. He retained the brass helmet of the Line dragoons, the only metal helmet of a Guard cavalry regiment. This uniform remained essentially unchanged throughout the life of the Empire.

The Guard commander, Marshal Bessières, who had little sympathy for this 'new' spirit, referred to Arrighi's Dragoons as *muscadins* (dandies). None the less, when their colonel presented two NCOs, dressed in the new uniform, to Napoleon in the palace at Saint-Cloud, the Emperor gave it his approval.

The red plume of this rider's helmet identifies him as a company officer. The black horse-hair queue of his helmet, emerging from beneath the covering plate of its crest, well forward toward the *porte-aigrette*, identifies it as the first model worn by the regiment. His saddle is covered with white leather. The single caps and skirts covering his pistol holsters would be replaced in 1808 by triple-layered hoods.

Dragoons of the Guard were never issued the smooth-legged, stiff boots worn in dress uniform by the Horse Grenadiers. Consequently, although he is in full dress, this officer's boots are of the semi-rigid type, with stiff knee sections only.

Garde Impériale ~ Dragons de l'Impératrice. 1806-1815.

Officier. Tenue de parade. 1806-1808.

Plate 43

Garde Impériale – Dragons de l'Impératrice. 1806–1815
Brigadier and Dragoons. Full dress. 1806–1808.

In this painting, we can see more clearly how the horse-hair queue of this model helmet rises very near its peak, then flows down over the sides of the crest and behind the rider's neck. While its function is primarily decorative, it also provides some protection against blows directed at a trooper's neck. The fur band around the helmet's base and over its visor are of simulated panther skin. (Officers' helmets may have had turbans of genuine panther skin.)

One change in the design of the *habit* was made soon after its adoption. In the first version, a small green triangle of cloth was visible below the point at which the scarlet *retroussis* met, sewn to the coat tail. This was eliminated by the redesign seen here on the *brigadier*'s *habit*. Initially, the Dragoons were issued with a *surtout* as an undress uniform coat, similar in cut to those worn by the Grenadiers. In 1809, however, they were issued two identical dress *habits* of the design seen here. One was reserved for dress purposes; the other, after a year's use, was worn during normal service and on campaign. (The *second habit* was sometimes still referred to as a *surtout*.) It was in the latter uniform that the Dragoons took part in the Russian campaign.

The original intention had been to mount the regiment on black horses, but Marshal Bessières instructed the commanding officer to procure bay or chestnut horses, pointing out that black horses were designated only for the Horse Grenadiers, the artillery and the *Gendarmes d'Elite*.

In October 1806, the first two squadrons to be formed proceeded to Prussia to join the cavalry of the *Grande Armée* in time for the Battle of Jena. On 27 October, they entered Berlin with the victors of Jena and Auerstaedt.

Garde Impériale - Dragons de l'Impératrice. 1806-1815.

Brigadier et dragons. Grande tenue. 1806 à 1808.

PLATE 44

Garde Impériale – Dragons de l'Impératrice. 1806–1815
Trumpeters. Full dress worn from 1806 to 1810.

The cut of the trumpeters' *habits* was identical to that of the troopers, although those shown here still have the free-floating *retroussis* before they were squared off at the bottom of the coat tails and sewn to them. The most striking difference is the substitution of sky-blue for the green of the rest of the regiment's *habits*. In addition, gold lace has been added to the cuffs, the collar, the edges of the *revers* (which now have gold lace buttonholes), the buttonholes of the pockets and the two buttons at the waist in the back of the coat. Three gold lace buttonholes appear below each lapel, and the gold-trimmed epaulettes are secured by gold lace straps. Each trumpeter's aiguillettes and the trumpet's cord are composed of a third gold thread and two-thirds sky-blue wool. The proportions are reversed for the trumpet-major, who wears on his sleeves the double gold stripes of a *maréchal-des-logis-chef*. The regiment's three *brigadiers-trompettes*, one of whom was attached to the *vélite* squadron, wear the single gold stripe of a *maréchal-des-logis*.

The trumpeters' helmets are of the same design as the troopers', although of finer quality. Their plumes are sky-blue, rather than red, and their queues and the tufts of the *porte-aigrettes* are of white horse hair. The trumpeters' saddle-cloths, holster covers and portmanteaus are of sky-blue cloth, trimmed with *aurore* braid.

On campaign, the trumpeters wore their *surtouts*. It seems likely that the splendid uniforms in this painting never left Paris.

When the regiment reached full strength in December 1807, its *fanfare* consisted of a trumpet-major, a *brigadier* kettledrummer, two *brigadier* trumpeters and twenty-four trumpeters.

L. Rousselot

Garde Impériale ⋅ Dragons de l'Impératrice. 1806-1815.

Trompettes . grande tenue portée de 1806 à 1810.

PLATE 45

Garde Impériale – Dragons de l'Impératrice, 1806–1815
Officer in march order, 1806–1809.

The almost sombre dress of this officer, in his green *surtout* and trousers, is echoed by the unadorned housing of his mount, both saddle-cloth and holster covers being trimmed with braid of woven goat's hair, colour on colour. But even in the absence of its tall red plume, his finely-worked helmet retains its glistening brilliance. Like so many of his fellow officers of the Guard cavalry, he is entitled to wear the ribbon of the Legion on his left breast.

During these four years, this officer and his men could be anywhere from Tilsit in the east to Madrid in the west. In early 1807, the squadrons that had arrived in Berlin in the previous October were employed in operations against partisans, who were harassing the French lines of communication. After participating in the battles of Eylau and Friedland, by November the regiment was back in Paris, finally at a full strength of five squadrons (one of these was made up of *vélites*), totalling eighty officers and 1296 men.

Early in 1808, the regiment joined other Guard cavalry regiments in Spain, where it participated in the battles of Medina-del-Rio-Seco, Benavente, Mayorga and Leon. With the Austrian campaign under way in the spring of 1809, the regiment was ordered to proceed to that theatre of operations.

On 22 May, 1500 Dragoons, under the command of Arrighi de Casanova, arrived in time to take part in the Battle of Aspern-Essling, after a march of 2800 km from Valladolid, Spain, without losing a man or a horse.

L. Rousselot

Garde Impériale - Dragons de l'Impératrice, 1806-1815.

Officier en tenue de route, 1806-1809.

Plate 46

Garde Impériale – Dragons de l'Impératrice
Maréchal-des-logis. Service full dress; *Maréchal-des-logis-chef* in quarters dress;
Fourrier in undress.

This scene may illustrate the first morning formation of a platoon of the duty squadron, prior to its forming up to relieve the guard at the Palace of Saint-Cloud. The *fourrier*, reading from his *Controle 1 Escadron* notebook, may be informing the *maréchal-des-logis-chef* of the troopers available for duty. His status as an NCO is confirmed by the single gold lace slash on his sleeve, the gold lace trim of his *bonnet de police* and its mixed gold and red wool piping and tassel, and his aiguillettes and *contre-epaulettes*. His non-regulation Souvorov-style boots were procured at his own expense.

The *grande tenue de service* worn by the *maréchal-des-logis* is appropriate for the type of duty we are assuming here. For convenience, prior to mounting up, he has tied his chin scales over the visor of his helmet. Given the design of the tails of his *habit*, which still display the green cloth triangle of the coat below the junction of the scarlet turn-backs, this scene must be taking place during the first years of the regiment's existence.

At this early stage of the day, the *maréchal-des-logis-chef* has left his own *contre-epaulettes* and aiguillettes in his quarters, the only decoration on his *redingote* being the ribbon of the Legion. NCOs obtained these coats at their own expense. His épée hangs from his dress belt, its guard dressed with a sword-knot of gold thread and red wool.

Garde Impériale ~ Dragons de l'Impératrice.

Maréchal-des-Logis. Grande tenue de service ; Maréchal-des-Logis-Chef en tenue de quartier.

Fourrier en petite tenue.

PLATE 47

Garde Impériale – Dragons de l'Impératrice. 1806–1815
Guard dressed in sentry's overcoat, 1806–1808.

In later years, a version of the caped coat worn by these sentries would be issued to all mounted Guard cavalrymen who, at this time, were still furnished with the sleeveless 'three-quarters' cloaks. Presumably the need for a sentry to handle his musket made the *capote*, with its small cape, more suitable for dismounted duties. It should be remembered that Dragoons were expected to be able to march and fight on foot. Two hundred Dragoons dispatched from the Paris depot to Berlin in late November 1806 were forced to make their way there on foot, for want of horses. Once there, they were given mounts taken from the King of Prussia's regiment of *Gensd'armes*.

The *brigadier* who is posting the sentries wears his waist-belt, with its bayonet scabbard and his sabre, over his shoulder *en baudrier*. The diamond-shaped, stamped brass plate ornamenting his *giberne* is decorated with a crowned shield bearing an eagle, while there is a star in each of its other corners.

We can see clearly how the horse-hair queue of each Dragoon's helmet emerges from beneath the plate covering the helmet's crest, near its peak, and falls down over its sides and to the rear.

It seems paradoxical that the red plumes of the Dragoons' helmets are worn at all, if the weather requires them to be encased in their oiled silk sleeves. But if the prescribed uniform for sentry duty called for plumes, then plumes would be worn. Perhaps this was done so that if the weather took a favourable turn, the sleeves could be removed promptly.

I. Rousselot

Garde Impériale – Dragons de l'Impératrice. 1806-1815.

Tenue de garde en capote de guérite. 1806-1808.

PLATE 48

Garde Impériale – Dragons de l'Impératrice. 1806–1815
Officer in morning walking-out dress and dragoons in walking-out dress.

Regulations for walking out, or 'going into town', dress took into account the time of year, day of the week and time of day. Winter ran from 1 October to 7 April, although summer dress regulations did not become effective until 1 May. Weekday dress was less elegant than Sunday dress and, as the artist's title for this officer indicates, morning dress and afternoon or evening dress also differed in some respects. In the latter case, the officer's black silk stockings would probably be replaced by white silk.

The setting for this scene appears to be the left bank of the Seine, across from the Place de la Concorde. If the autumn foliage and the fur collar of the young lady's very *à la mode* coat don't make it clear, the officer's green breeches tell us that the first of October has arrived. A white dress collar rises from within the collar of his *surtout*, upon which he wears the Star of the Legion, rather than simply its ribbon. It may be because of Arrighi's attempt to eliminate 'frills' that the dragoons' *chapeaux* carry only a single gold lace strap, which holds in place the hat's cockade, and that they are not decorated at each corner by tassels.

The gallant dragoons have pulled their Souvorov boots over their deerskin breeches and, having removed the bayonet scabbards, have slung their waist-belts over their right shoulders *en baudrier*. Each belt buckle carries a crowned shield, which bears an eagle with wings deployed.

L. Rousselot

Garde Impériale ≈ Dragons de l'Impératrice 1806-1815.

Officier en tenue de sortie du matin et Dragons en tenue de ville.

PLATE 49

Garde Impériale – Dragons de l'mpératrice. 1806–1815
Walking-out dress. *Maréchal-des-logis-chef*, in dress coat, and *fourrier* in undress coat.

Again, because of these NCOs' dress, we may assume that this scene takes place during the winter season. In this instance, Rousselot has given us an almost schematic depiction of the back of a *sous-officier's surtout*, and of the front of another *sous-officier's habit*. This allows us to see more clearly the manner in which gold thread and scarlet wool are woven together respectively in the one-to-two ratio for the *fourrier's* aiguillettes and sword-knot, and in the opposite ratio for the *maréchal-des-logis-chef's* accessories.

The comparatively modest appearance of their *chapeaux* is equally evident. They are wearing their large hats in the approved fashion, the right corner being advanced 45 degrees from the shoulder line. This is a compromise between the *en bataille* position (parallel with the shoulders) and the *en colonne* position (straight fore-and-aft).

In another concession to convention, the *maréchal-des-logis-chef* has left unbuttoned two of his cuff buttons. The design of the men's Souvorov-style boots, rising to a point in the rear, is noteworthy.

A sharp eye will have spotted the print of Napoleon, as well as its companion piece, a print of a Napoleonic infantry officer. Soldiers sought out prints illustrating soldiers of their own type, which they sent home to their families. Some regiments had special stationary printed for their men, bearing naïve coloured images of Napoleon or of a representative soldier of their own regiment.

Garde Impériale : Dragons de l'Impératrice. 1806-1815

Tenues de ville . Maréchal-des-logis-chef, en habit et fourrier en surtout.

Plate 50

Garde Impériale – Dragons de l'Impératrice. 1806–1815
Officers in society dress and *redingote*.

The *habit* of the officer who is preparing for an evening's festivities is that of his parade dress uniform, but the remainder of his attire – his silk (or nankeen) breeches, silk stockings, silver-buckled shoes, black stock and white shirt collar – is reserved for such occasions as this. His *redingote* has been put aside, and his pearl-handled dress *épée de ville* will soon be hanging at his side. His dress hat, lying nearby, is adorned with gold thread tassels at each corner.

Perhaps his fellow officer is on duty this evening, since he is wearing gloves and is still in his *redingote*, dressed with his aiguillettes and epaulettes.

The officer's *ordonnance*, a trooper of the regiment, is in his stable jacket and side-buttoned drill trousers. According to Lachouque, Guard officers were required to have *domestiques* – personal servants. Those wishing to employ civilians needed the approval of the regiment's commanding officer. Such servants may have been required to dress in a semblance of a uniform for purposes of identification. Officers of means could assemble a considerable personal staff to support them, both at the regimental depot in Paris and in the field.

The luxury of the apartment in which these officers appear to be quartered suggests that they are in Paris. The swan, which the artist has worked into the carved wood panelling, is a tribute to the Empress Josephine, the 'god-mother' of the regiment, whose symbol it was.

Garde Impériale ~ Dragons de l'"Impératrice. 1806-1815.

Officiers en tenue de société et en redingote.

PLATE 51

Garde Impériale – Dragons de l'Impératrice. 1806–1815
Dragoons and trumpeter in cloaks. Campaigns of 1806 and 1807.

It may be recalled that, late in 1806, the regiment had begun to come together in Berlin, and early in the following year, it had been given responsibility for thwarting efforts by bands of Prussian partisans to disrupt the French lines of communication. The scene that Rousselot presents in this painting could well represent men of the regiment engaged in those operations.

Since many of the officers of the regiment, as well as the majority of the men – with the exception of the *vélite* squadron – had come from the draft on the thirty line Dragoon regiments, they were familiar with, if not masters of, their trade. None the less, they needed the discipline of working together as a regiment, and this task afforded them that training. Their first fully-fledged experience in battle was to come at Friedland, in June that year. It was only at the end of 1807, however, that the regiment attained its full strength.

The men in this painting are wearing their 'three-quarters' cloaks, which are ample enough to cover the horse as well as the rider, protecting the housing and permitting the men to benefit from their horses' body heat. The scarlet serge panels do not line the entire garment, but only narrow sections inside both front openings and the shorter vent at the rear. The dark green collars of the Dragoons' cloaks and the sky-blue collar of the trumpeter's cloak echo the colours of their uniform coats.

Garde Impériale ~ Dragons de l'Impératrice, 1806-1815.

Dragons et trompette en manteau. Campagnes de 1806 et 1807.

PLATE 52

Garde Impériale – Dragons de l'Impératrice. 1806–1815
Maréchal-des-logis and dragoons, march order, 1807–1808.

In May 1807, the regiment had been ordered to join the Imperial General Headquarters, which Napoleon had established at Finkenstein. There he reviewed the Dragoons on 28 May. At the Battle of Friedland, on 14 June, the regiment was posted on the left flank of the Guard cavalry, and that evening it participated in the pursuit of the Russians.

Judging by the design of the houses in the background of this painting, the regiment was still in eastern Europe. After accompanying the Guard cavalry to Tilsit with the Emperor, the regiment joined the *Grande Armée* in its triumphal entry to Paris in November, all regiments being in campaign uniforms at the express instructions of Napoleon. Not having participated in the campaign of 1805 and, for that matter, not yet having received an eagle, the regiment was not awarded one of the golden wreaths presented to other regiments by the City of Paris.

These Dragoons are in their *surtouts* and duck overalls. The single hoods and skirts over their pistol holsters will be replaced in 1808 by a triple-layered design. The artist shows us clearly the method of carrying the troopers' muskets: the butt end of the weapon rests in a leather boot, while its muzzle is restrained by a strap attached to the saddle's pommel. The Grenadiers used a similar arrangement, while the Chasseurs carried their carbines in the reverse position – muzzle down, butt close to the elbow. The *Chevau-légers* did the same until they were armed with the lance, after which the carbine was carried on the near-side of the horse.

Garde Impériale ~ Dragons de l'Impératrice. 1806-1815.

Maréchal-des-logis et dragons, tenue de route, 1807-1808.

PLATE 53

Garde Impériale – Dragons de l'Impératrice. 1806–1815
Trumpeters, guard dress and walking-out dress in undress coat. 1806–1810.
Dragoons, the same dress worn until 1815.

In a break from his customary manner of providing sub-titles for his paintings, in this instance Rousselot has separated its subjects into two periods, that of the trumpeters concluding in 1810. That was the year of Napoleon's marriage to Marie-Louise, which caused a considerable sprucing-up of the Guard and its uniforms. Among those whose uniforms were most strikingly affected were the trumpeters of the Dragoons, as can be seen in Plate 57. In contrast, the uniforms of the regiment's troopers remained fundamentally unchanged during the life of the Empire.

The trumpeter on guard duty is in his *surtout* and sheepskin breeches, his sword belt worn over the shoulder *en baudrier*. (Dragoons, trumpeters and troopers alike, were issued breeches of sheared sheepskin, trousers of deerskin, overalls of cotton drill and stable trousers of duck.) His fellow duty dragoon is dressed in the same manner, having put on his *banderole* and *giberne*, since he is under arms. If he is presenting arms to a distinguished passenger in the *post chaise* in the background, the other Dragoons are oblivious of, or indifferent to, that fact.

The trumpeter and dragoon in conversation are in their weekday, winter *tenues de ville*, the trooper with his sabre, while the trumpeter's épée hangs from his dress sword-belt at his side.

Garde Impériale « Dragons de l'Impératrice. 1806 1815.

Trompettes, tenue de garde et tenue de ville en surtout. 1806 à 1810.

Dragons, mêmes tenues portées jusqu'en 1815.

PLATE 54

Garde Impériale – Dragons de l'Impératrice. 1806–1815
Campaign dress in dress coat. 1808–1809.

When he executed this painting, Rousselot may have had in mind the Battle of Aspern-Essling on 21–22 May, in which the Dragoons distinguished themselves. However, this inconclusive engagement served as a prelude to the decisive French victory at Wagram on 5–6 July 1809, in which the regiment also performed notably.

In the period between those battles, the 'founding' officer of the regiment, Arrighi de Casanova, was replaced by General Count Bonardi de Saint-Sulpice, a cuirassier commander who had been the Emperor's Master of the Horse. Arrighi, in turn, replaced General d'Espagne, killed at Essling, as commander of the latter's cuirassier division.

In their campaign uniforms, the Dragoons in this painting are wearing their 'second' *habits* and their *surculottes* (overalls) of cotton drill, fastened on the outside of each leg by sixteen bone buttons. Their cloaks are tied over their shoulders and chests for additional protection, and their muskets are slung on their backs in a less encumbering position than when hung from the saddle at their right side.

These troopers are galloping in a relatively loose formation, which suggests that the initial charge of the squadron, which would have been carried out in as close to a straight line abreast as possible, has already taken place. It is likely that the order for the pursuit of a broken enemy formation has been given by the squadron commander.

Garde Impériale ~ Dragons de l'Impératrice. 1806-1815.

Tenue de campagne en habit 1808-1809.

PLATE 55

Garde Impériale – Dragons de l'Impératrice. 1806–1815
Senior officer. Full dress. 1810–1815.

Two immediately obvious features of this Dragoon's appearance confirm his status as a senior officer: the white plume of his helmet and the three bands of gold lace framing the saddle cloth and holster covers of his mount's housing. White plumes were worn by *chefs d'escadron*, adjutants and members of the regimental headquarters staff. A colonel's plume was taller and made from vulture feathers.

Soon after Arrighi had begun to organise the regiment, he received a sharp note from Bessières, then the Guard commander, pointing out that Napoleon's instructions for the uniforms of the regiment had specified red plumes, and asking Arrighi by virtue of what order his regiment had adopted white plumes. The latter's response was short and to the point: 'Fantasy!' Apparently, being a cousin of the Emperor gave him a sense of invulnerability to the 'slings and arrows' of lesser mortals, even marshals. (None the less, the Dragoon troopers' plumes ended up being red.)

Grande tenue (full dress) required the horse's undress black leather snaffle-bridle to be exchanged for one of woven gold thread, and its forelock to be braided with red wool and, along with the crupper, decorated with red ribbon rosettes. The saddle's undress surcingle has been replaced with a white, striped version. The saddle itself is covered in white lacquered leather.

The design of the Dragoon helmet, for both officers and men, was slightly modified in about 1810 by shifting further towards the rear of the crest the point at which the horse-hair queue emerged.

Garde Impériale - Dragons de l'Impératrice. 1806-1815.

Officier supérieur. Grande tenue. 1810-1815.

Plate 56

Garde Impériale – Dragons de l'Impératrice. 1806–1815
Kettledrummer about 1810.

The history of kettledrummers in the French Army can be traced back at least to Louis XIV, who presented kettledrums to all of the Household Cavalry except the Musketeers. Such drums were abolished during the Revolution, but ten years later, Napoleon, as First Consul, reintroduced them for the *Grenadiers à cheval* and the *Chasseurs à cheval* of the Consular Guard. When the *Dragons* were formed in 1806, they were authorised a *timbalier*.

The first costume of the Dragoon's *timbalier* bore no resemblance to that depicted in Rousselot's painting. That *timbalier*'s turban was green, his *yalek* (sleeveless over-vest) crimson, his *charoual* (loose trousers) green, and his drum banners dragoon green, with alternating gold eagles and crowns.

With the uniforms of the regiment's trumpeters having been redesigned in preparation for the festivities surrounding the marriage of Napoleon and Marie-Louise, it was logical that the *timbalier*'s should match. Thus his white, gold lace-trimmed *yalek* complements the *habits* of the trumpeters. The sky-blue drum banners now bear the Imperial coat of arms,

In the text for his *Planche* No. 53, Rousselot states that the archives contain no information on this uniform. Therefore, his painting, apparently done prior to the *planche*, was based primarily on the Alsatian paper soldiers, which portray the drummer as black. However, his text for the *planche* states that the three successive *timbaliers* of the regiment had been identified as being white. Indeed, thirty-two years later, the artist said that he had learned that the kettledrummer in 1810 had been a Frenchman, as were his three successors.

Garde Impériale ~ Dragons de l'Impératrice : 1806-1815.

Timbalier vers 1810.

PLATE 57

Garde Impériale – Dragons de l'Impératrice. 1806–1815
Trumpeters. Parade uniform. 1810–1814.

The predominantly white colour of the trumpeters' new parade uniforms is thought to have been a tribute to the Emperor's new bride, whose upbringing in the Austrian court would have made the white coats of her father's army a familiar sight to her. These coats, for ceremonial parade occasions, were laden with even more gold lace than the sky-blue *habits* they replaced. Given the fragility of these luxurious uniforms, it seems probable that the other dress *habits* were retained for wear on less important occasions. Rousselot wonders whether there might even have been a somewhat less elegant white *habit* for 'ordinary' parades, but there is no proof of this.

The only known surviving example of a Dragoon trumpeter's helmet confirms that the design of the crest of the helmet is as Rousselot shows it on the trumpeter with his back to the viewer. Its queue emerges from beneath the crest's cover-plate, near the lower end of the crest.

Both sides of the trumpet banners are of the same design as those of the *Grenadiers à cheval*. For parade dress, the horses have their forelocks braided with sky-blue wool cord and decorated with rosettes; similar rosettes, with sky-blue and gold ribbons, are attached to their cruppers.

L. Rousselot

Garde Impériale ː Dragons de l'Impératrice ﹒1806﹣1815

Trompettes ﹣ Tenue de parade   1810 ﹣ 1814﹒

PLATE 58

Garde Impériale – Dragons de l'Impératrice. 1806–1815
Brigadier-trompette in walking-out dress. Trumpeter and troopers in stable dress.

This scene emphasises the fact that, underlying the splendour of the regiment's appearance on parade, were countless hours of grooming of the troopers' mounts, and policing of their stables and yard. The simple stable jacket of the trumpeter wielding the broom is at the opposite end of the military dress spectrum from his splendid gold-lace-trimmed *habit*.

Two details of the uniforms shown in this painting suggest that the scene is set at least in 1812. One is the white piping along the edge of the *aurore* braid on the *bonnet de police* of the trumpeter in stable dress, a modification that was introduced in about 1812, according to Rousselot's text for his *Planche* No. 53. The other is the collar of the *brigadier-trompette*'s *surtout*, which previously had been sky-blue, but which became crimson at the time of the major changes in the trumpeters' uniforms in 1810.

An indication of the somewhat superior status of a *brigadier-trompette* compared to a *brigadier* trooper, is that the former was entitled to wear a gold lace rank stripe and the mixed gold and wool aiguillettes of an NCO. A *brigadier* trooper was not considered an NCO.

In combat, trumpeters were expected to – and did – use their sabres to good effect. In close quarters, they often assisted in the protection of their commanding officers, by whose side they were required to remain.

L. Rousselot

Garde Impériale ⋉ *Dragons de l'Impératrice* 1806-1815

Brigadier-trompette en tenue de ville. Trompette et cavaliers en tenue d'écurie.

PLATE 59

Garde Impériale – Dragons de l'Impératrice. 1806–1815
Parade uniform 1810 for the celebrations of the marriage with the
Archduchess Marie-Louise.

Although now there would be a new *Impératrice*, in the hearts and minds of the men of the regiment there would still be only one Empress. As long as any of the regiment survived, they would make an annual pilgrimage to her grave on the anniversary of her death. There was irony in the fact that this new Empress was an Austrian, rekindling memories of the wife of an earlier monarch, the much vilified and condemned Marie Antoinette.

The civil marriage ceremony took place in the palace at Saint-Cloud on 1 April. At noon on 2 April 1810, the procession wound its way down the Champs Elysées toward the Louvre. There, in the chapel, the religious ceremony would take place. The Coronation in Notre Dame would follow.

The glittering panoply of the Empire at its apogee was on full display. Here, the Coronation coach has just passed beneath a triumphal arch celebrating the marriage and is entering the Garden of the Tuileries. The *Chevau-légers Polonais*, the *Chasseurs à cheval* and the Mameluks preceded the Coronation coach, the immediate escort of which was provided by the *Dragons de l'Impératrice*, while the *Grenadiers à cheval* followed close behind.

The Dragoons have put aside their portmanteaus, but have retained their folded cloaks, which are secured to the cantles of their saddles. Parade rosettes are attached to their horses' braided forelocks and cruppers.

Garde Impériale - Dragons de l'Impératrice 1806-1815.

Tenue de parade 1810. aux fêtes du mariage avec l'Archiduchesse Marie-Louise.

PLATE 60

Garde Impériale – Dragons de l'Impératrice. 1806–1815
Eagle-bearer lieutenant. 1811–1813.

In 1808, Minister of War Clarke informed Napoleon that the Dragoons, whose organisation included four *porte-aigles*, wished to receive guidons for the regiment. He received a reply on 17 August, which stated that the regiment would receive its guidons when it was fully formed. It was not until 15 August 1811, however, at a parade in honour of the Emperor's birthday, that the regiment received, not its guidons, but a single eagle. On 31 August, the Guard administrative council requested a standard (*sic*) for the eagle. There is no record of the response to that request.

A guidon of the 1804 design in a private collection bears on its reverse side the inscription Rousselot shows in this painting: '*GARDE IMPÉRIALE*'; '*VALEUR ET DISCIPLINE*'; '*1er ESCADRON*'. The inscription on the obverse reads, '*L'EMPEREUR DES FRANÇAIS AU RÉGIMENT DE DRAGONS DE L'IMPÉRATRICE*'. The laurel wreaths in its corners contain flaming grenades.

General Regnault and Pierre Charrié speculate that Napoleon may have refused to grant the guidon because it bore the title '*Dragons de l'Impératrice*', which had never been made official, notwithstanding its common usage. He may also have objected to the fact that the words '*Garde Impériale*' were on the reverse of the guidon, rather than the obverse, as was the case with the standards.

In the court of the Carrousel on 15 February 1813, the regiment received an 1812 model standard. The gold letters on its obverse read, '*GARDE IMPÉRIALE L'EMPEREUR NAPOLÉON AU RÉGIMENT DES DRAGONS*'. It seems probable that the inscriptions on the reverse would have been '*FRIEDLAND ECKMÜHL ESSLING VIENNE WAGRAM MADRID SMOLENSK MOSKOWA MOSCOU*'.

Garde Impériale ⤳ Dragons de l'Impératrice. 1806-1815

Lieutenant Porte-Aigle — 1811-1813.

I. Rousselot

PLATE 61

Garde Impériale – Dragons de l'Impératrice. 1806–1815
Campaign dress. 1812.

The regiment set out for the Russian campaign in several separate detachments and at different times. Its overall strength was sixty-four officers and 1022 men; half of their number would not see France again. In January 1812, a detachment left Paris, joining the squadrons under General Letort at Hanover. On 10 August, at Vitebsk, they were met by 400 troopers, who had come from Spain.

Perhaps when he painted this scene, Rousselot imagined those Dragoons somewhere between Vitebsk and Smolensk. The troopers are wearing their 'second' *habits* and their side-buttoned overalls, while the officers watching their men ford the stream have put on their *surtouts* and green breeches, having exchanged their dress schabraques and holster hoods for those edged with dark green braid.

Although the regiment was not heavily engaged as a whole en route to Moscow, *Colonel-major* Pinteville was wounded at Borodino, and two squadron commanders were killed in advanced post operations around Moscow. It was during the retreat from that city, however, that the regiment particularly distinguished itself. Its duty squadron participated in the skirmish with cossacks on the day after the battle, when Napoleon narrowly escaped capture.

In reporting that affair, Armand Caulaincourt observed, 'In no other army can the duties of reconnaissance have been so neglected.' Writing later of Malojaroslavets, General Philippe de Ségur referred to it as 'that fatal field, where the conquest of the world ended.'

Garde Impériale ~ Dragons de l'Impératrice 1806-1815.

Tenue de campagne -1812 -

PLATE 62

Garde Impériale – Dragons de l'Impératrice. 1806-1815
General of Division Count Ornano. Commanding the regiment from 1813 to 1815.

On 21 January 1813, Napoleon gave command of the regiment to another of his cousins, General of Division Count Philippe Antoine Ornano. (Saint-Sulpice had been named governor of Fontainebleau after the Russian campaign.) Following the Battle of Borodino, Ornano had been promoted to lieutenant-general. During the retreat from Moscow, he had been left for dead on the battlefield of Krasnoye, and since had made a painful recovery. Now he was given the task of rebuilding the shattered regiment.

Within a month, with a new call for men he had set on foot five squadrons, to which Napoleon ordered the addition of a sixth, of 300 men in two companies. This squadron was called the 2nd Regiment, or the 2nd Dragoons. Its men were termed *cavaliers seconds*, classified as Young Guard, and given Line pay and subsistence. Ornano's commandants were General Letort and General Pinteville, the latter being put in charge of the 2nd Dragoons.

Here Ornano is shown at a dress parade in the Place du Carrousel, before leaving Paris with his reconstituted regiment for Germany. Already a commander of the *Légion d'Honneur*, on 13 April he had been awarded the *Grand Croix de l'Order de la Réunion*, the embroidered plaque of which can be seen on his breast.

In May, the Guard cavalry was organised into two divisions: a light division, under Lefèbvre-Desnouëttes, consisting of the *Chevau-légers* of the 1st and 2nd Regiments and the Berg Lancers; and a heavy division, under Ornano, comprising the Chasseurs, Dragoons, Grenadiers and 500 Elite Gendarmes.

Garde Impériale x Dragons de l'Impératrice 1806-1815.

Le Général de Division Comte Ornano. Commandant le Régiment de 1813 à 1815.

PLATE 63

Garde Impériale – Dragons de l'Impératrice. 1806–1815
Campaign dress in caped overcoat. 1813–1814.

The cloak-overcoats worn by the Dragoons in this painting, which were introduced in 1813, had capes that were somewhat longer than those of the cloak-coats they replaced. They were decorated in front with three *aurore* wool brandenburgs ending in tassels, those on the left having buttonholes, and those on the right, large uniform buttons. A vent in the left side of this *manteau-capote* afforded access to the trooper's sabre when the garment was closed.

With drawn sabres and muskets slung on their backs, these Dragoons appear to be awaiting their officer's command to go into action. The year 1813 put the regiment, and the entire army, to a steady succession of severe tests. The regiment's first action took place on 2 May at Lützen, and it was engaged in a second French victory, at Bautzen, on 20 May.

During an armistice, which was to have run from 4 June to 15 August, the Guard cavalry was reorganised again. This time, there were three divisions. The 1st, under Ornano, contained the Berg Lancers, Colbert's 2nd Light Horse and Pinteville's Young Guard Dragoons. The 2nd, commanded by Lefèbvre-Desnouëttes, had Krasinski's Young Guard squadrons of Polish Lancers and Chasseurs, and Castex's Grenadiers. The 3rd Division, led by General Walther, consisted of the Old Guard squadrons of Lion's Chasseurs, Letort's Dragoons and Laferrière's Grenadiers. The overall Guard cavalry commander was General Count Étienne Nansouty.

The peace was broken on 11 August, when Blücher took the offensive. On the 15th, Napoleon left Dresden and by the 18th the entire Guard was with him at Gorlitz, as the campaign resumed.

I. Rousselot

Garde Impériale ~ Dragons de l'Impératrice 1806-1815.

Tenue de campagne en manteau-capote. 1813-1814.

PLATE 64

Garde Impériale – Dragons de l'Impératrice. 1806–1815
Trumpeters. Campaign dress – 1813–1814.

By the early autumn of 1813, Napoleon had led the army to a series of victories, but none was sufficiently decisive to bring the campaign to a successful conclusion. Battlefield attrition continued to diminish the Emperor's forces, while the manpower resources of the Coalition powers seemed limitless. At this stage, the Guard made up a third of the French Army in the field, the cavalry under Nansouty totalling 483 officers and 7735 men.

We may imagine this scene taking place during a late afternoon bivouac, somewhere between Wachau and Leipzig. At the former, on 16 October the regiment had delivered successful charges against Russian Guards and Austrian cuirassiers, while at the latter, the fateful 'Battle of Nations' would take place during the following three days.

The only new elements in the men's uniforms are their grey overalls, which have replaced the side-buttoned cotton drill trousers. For some reason, Rousselot has not given the trumpeter's *manteau-capote* the three *aurore* brandenburgs that he describes in the text for his *Planche* No. 13. Its sky-blue collar, however, distinguishes it from the cloak-coats of the *cavaliers* of the regiment, which have green collars. The crimson collars, *retroussis*, cuffs and piping on the pockets of the trumpeters' *surtouts* date from the changes in their uniforms made at the time of the Emperor's marriage in 1810 .

Garde Impériale ✗ Dragons de l'Impératrice. 1806-1815.

Trompettes. Tenue de campagne — 1813 - 1814.

Plate 65

Garde Impériale – Dragons de l'Impératrice. 1806–1815
Officer and dragoons in cloaks. 1813–1814.

The retreat of the French Army after its shattering defeat at Leipzig reminded some of the men of the retreat from Moscow, even if the weather was somewhat better.

At Hanau on 30 October, Napoleon employed the infantry and cavalry of the Guard to break through the blockade thrown across the road back to France by the Bavarians, who had defected. Although their action succeeded, it was at a heavy cost. Among the cavalry casualties were General Letort's two majors and eight other officers. By 1 November, the bulk of the army had reached Frankfurt, and two days later it was in Mainz. Ornano's division, which had been left briefly in Kassel, followed five days later. To the exhausted and dysentery-ridden men of the army, seeing French territory across the Rhine must have made them feel as though they had reached the Promised Land.

In this painting, Rousselot has managed to convey the stoic endurance and unshakeable determination to persevere that characterised the men of the Guard in the face of the daunting odds that confronted the army as it made its way westward. Perhaps the officer is attempting to decipher a scrawled movement order brought to him by one of Nansouty's aides.

The fact that the troopers do not have leather lock-covers strapped to their muskets suggests that they are prepared for, if not expecting, action. The ungroomed horses indicate the exhausting pace that the army has been forced to maintain.

Although Rousselot describes these soldiers as being *en manteau*, they are actually wearing caped over-coats.

I. Rousselot

Garde Impériale ~ Dragons de l'Impératrice. 1806-1815.

Officier et dragons en manteau. 1813-1814.

PLATE 66

Garde Impériale – Dragons de l'Impératrice. 1806–1815
Uniform of the Young Guard squadrons. 1813–1814. Only officers,
NCOs and trumpeters wore aiguillettes.

Possibly one of Napoleon's most brilliant improvisations was his creation of the Young Guard. While the men of these regiments and squadrons lacked combat skills and experience, these shortcomings were outweighed by their pride in being part of the most prestigious military formation of the age, and by a fervent desire to demonstrate that they were worthy of fighting alongside their 'elders'. During the three months of the Campaign of France, the Young Guard had many opportunities to do so, and they measured up in every instance.

As Napoleon employed the full range of his strategic and tactical skills to stave off the inevitable, his troops survived a continuous succession of skirmishes and pitched battles, separated only by night and forced marches in punishing weather. At times, the Dragoons and Grenadiers travelled on foot, pulling their horses out of foot-deep mud by their muzzles. But the Dragoons were present at every battle: Langres, Bar-sur-Aube, Montmirail, Château-Thierry, Champaubert, Craonne, Laon, Arcis-sur-Aube and, finally, the battle for Paris.

On 12 February, when the Prussian Army was blocking the route to Château-Thierry, Napoleon ordered the Guard cavalry into action against the enemy's right flank. Led by Letort's Young Guard Dragoons, the cavalry swept down on the squares of Prussian infantry, smashing one, then two others. The duty squadrons helped drive the Prussians back into Château-Thierry and across the Marne bridge.

That evening, the Emperor awarded Letort a third Star of the Legion.

I. Rousselot

Garde Impériale ∞ Dragons de l'Impératrice 1806-1815.

Tenue des escadrons de Jeune-Garde. 1813-1814.

Les officiers, sous officiers et trompettes portaient seuls les aiguillettes.

PLATE 67

Garde Impériale – Chevau-légers Polonais. 1807–1814
Trumpeters, full dress. 1807–1809.

The most reliable evidence for the design of the first uniforms worn by the regiment's trumpeters comes from the memoirs of General Count Josef Zaluski, an officer with the *Chevau-légers Polonais*. Apart from the striking all-crimson image that these men presented, the cut of their uniforms was identical to that of the regiment's troopers. Silver lace bordered the white *revers*, collars and cuffs of their *kurtkas* (short-tailed jacket), while the piping along the seams and outlining the pockets of the *kurtka* was of white cord. Their aiguillettes, fringed and trefoil epaulettes, and the cords of their *schapskas* (square-topped caps) and trumpets were woven from a third silver thread and two-thirds white thread. All metal elements of the uniform, other than the belt buckle and portions of the *schapska* plate, were silvered, as was the metal of the horse's harness.

The sabres and pistols issued to the regiment upon its formation were primarily drawn from captured Prussian stocks, generally being of indifferent quality. The sabres worn by the trumpeters in this painting would later be replaced by the same type that equipped the Guard Chasseurs.

When en route, the trumpeters' crimson trousers were replaced by leather-reinforced, dark blue over-alls, which had white metal buttons along a crimson stripe on the outside of the leg. The white *revers* of the *kurtka* were turned under, and their crimson lining exposed. The *schapska* was covered by its black oiled silk cover, and its plume stowed in the portmanteau.

Garde Impériale ~ Chevau-légers Polonais. 1807-1814.

Trompettes, grande tenue. 1807-1809.

PLATE 68

Garde Impériale – Chevau-légers Polonais. 1807–1814
Full dress. 1807 to 1809.

Soon after the formation of the regiment, at a review conducted before the Emperor, its squadrons became so entangled with one another that Napoleon exclaimed impatiently, 'These young fellows don't know anything!' Dismissing their two French instructors, he ordered one of his aides to take them in hand. Two months later, they had been 'civilised', but at a subsequent review at Schönbrunn, the regiment's performance bordered on disaster. In disgust, the Emperor upbraided all concerned, commenting, 'These people only know how to fight!' They would prove that soon afterwards, at Somosierra and Wagram.

A unique feature of the men's *kurtkas* was the silver lace bordering the jacket's crimson *revers*. NCOs' collars and cuffs were also trimmed with silver lace. The uniform trousers were given their snug fit by five crimson cord loops, starting at the level of the fleshy part of the calf and woven though one another, the fifth being looped around a button at the bottom of the trouser leg. This, in turn, was attached to a strap passing under the boot.

For full dress, a double white cord, from which hung a tassel and two flounders, was wound around the *schapska*. At this time, the troopers' carbines were slung on the right side of their saddles, muzzle down. One of the joined *banderoles* carried the *giberne*, while a steel clip on the second supported the carbine when it had been freed for action.

The regiment's horses were grouped in squadrons by the colour of their coats: chestnut, bay, black or dark grey. They stood 14¼–14¾ hands high and would be five or six years old when purchased.

Garde Impériale ᵪ Chevau-légers Polonais. 1807-1814.

Grande tenue . 1807 à 1809.

PLATE 69

Garde Impériale – Chevau-légers Polonais. 1807–1814
March order. 1807–1809.

To protect the silver-trimmed crimson *revers* of the *kurtka*, in marching order they were folded beneath the opposing dark blue *revers*, the edge of which was trimmed with crimson piping. The troopers' tight dress trousers were replaced by looser travelling trousers (*pantalon de voyage*), reinforced between the legs and around their bottoms with black leather. Eighteen pewter buttons were placed along a strip of crimson cloth on the outer seam of each leg. The troopers' *schapskas* were enclosed in waxed cloth covers. Their dress trousers would be folded beneath their portmanteaus and the *sac à distribution* (feed bag). (Commandant Bucquoy states that when the regiment marched from their depot in Chantilly to Spain early in 1808, the men were in their stable jackets and side-buttoned cotton drill trousers.)

When the regiment returned to France from Spain in March 1809, it received new arms, including light cavalry sabres of the Year XI model with steel scabbards. When the weight of the latter provoked many complaints, sabres of the hussar, or *Chasseurs de la Garde*, type, with wooden scabbards covered with leather and brass, were issued, as can be seen in this painting.

Since it was evident, when the first squadrons of the regiment arrived in Spain, that the men needed field combat experience, General Lasalle was entrusted with the task of affording them that experience. He did so by employing them on outpost duties. One of the regiment's officers wrote of him, 'It was in General Lasalle's school that we learned outpost duty. We have kept a precious memory of this general, in whom all the lovable and imposing qualities of a born marshal were combined.'

L. Rousselot

Garde Impériale ~ Chevau-légers Polonais. 1807-1814.

Tenue de route   1807-1809.

PLATE 70

Garde Impériale – Chevau-légers Polonais. 1807–1814
Maréchal-des-logis and troopers of the service squadron. Somosierra. 1808.

This painting commemorates an episode in the history of the regiment that would be associated with its name forever. In late November 1808, Napoleon, with Victor's corps, the Guard and the cavalry reserve, was en route from Burgos to Madrid. On the 29th, this small army was stopped at a pass through the Guadarrama range by Spanish troops and armed peasants, supported by sixteen guns in four batteries.

Irritated at being held up, Napoleon ordered a direct assault up the road to the pass. General Piré, commanding the cavalry of the advance guard, protested that such an attack was impossible. Napoleon's harsh reply was, 'Impossible? I do not know the meaning of that word!' Turning to Major Baron Kozietulski, the commander of the *Chevau-légers* duty squadron, he said, 'Here's an opportunity for you to earn your spurs, Monsieur. Clear that road for me, and quickly!'

Two attempts by the squadron to clear the road failed, with heavy losses of officers and men. Finally, Napoleon ordered General Montbrun to lead the regiment in a third assault, which he did successfully.

As Napoleon passed the scene of the fiercest engagement, he saw the wounded Lieutenant Niegolewski being tended by the side of the road. Leaning over him, the Emperor pinned his own Star of the Legion on the officer. The next day, he awarded sixteen more Stars to the *Chevau-légers* – eight to officers and eight to troopers. Taking his hat off to the regiment, he said, 'You are worthy of my Old Guard! Honour to the bravest of the brave!'

Since theirs was the duty squadron, the *maréchal-des-logis* and his men have uncovered the crimson *revers* of their *kurtkas* and affixed the plumes and dress cords to their *schapskas*.

L. Rousselot

Garde Impériale ~ Chevau-légers Polonais. 1807-1814.

Maréchal des logis et chevau-légers de l'escadron de service.

Jomo-Sierra. 1808.

PLATE 71

Garde Impériale – Chevau-légers Polonais. 1807–1814
Senior officer. Parade uniform. (This uniform was worn during the entire
existence of the Corps.)

With this painting, we have arrived at the point in the regiment's history when, with the addition of the lance to its armament, it has become the *Chevau-légers lanciers Polonais*. An immediate and very evident effect of this development on the regiment's uniforms was the shift of the troopers' aiguillettes from the right to the left shoulder, as a practical measure. Officers continued to wear their aiguillettes on the right shoulder, however.

The uniforms of the regiment's officers were among the most resplendent of any in the Guard – and ruinously expensive for the less affluent of the younger officers, petty nobility though they may have been. Since only the colonel and *colonels-majors* wore fringed epaulettes on both shoulders, the officer in this painting is presumably a *chef d'escadron*.

Such an officer's wardrobe would probably include one or two additional *kurtkas*, one of which would have dark blue lapels, bordered only with crimson piping, but retaining silver lace on the collar, cuffs and *retroussis*. It is also likely that he would have several extra pairs of trousers, several *habits*, a *redingote*, and a white, lace-trimmed *kurtka* and silk breeches for important social occasions.

Although the wearing of crimson trousers in full dress was usually restricted to senior officers, an order by *Colonel-major* Dautancourt on 30 August 1810 prescribed crimson trousers and belts or sashes for all officers on that occasion. A second, narrow row of silver lace, inside the larger band on the schabraque, was a distinction enjoyed by senior officers. While portmanteaus would not normally be carried in *tenue de parade*, a special order may have prescribed them on this occasion.

L. Rousselot

PLATE 72

Garde Impériale – Chevau-légers Polonais. 1807–1814
Senior officer. Full dress parade uniform.

A *grande parade* would be called for on special occasions such as Imperial events – the Emperor's birthday, for example – or receptions for foreign royalty or Imperial dignitaries, or even when entering a city. This one takes place on the *Champ de Mars*, with the *École Militaire* in the immediate background and the dome of the *Hôtel des Invalides* looming in the distance.

When the regiment was formed in Warsaw during the summer of 1807, the intention was to issue all the officers with white dress *kurtkas* of the type worn by the officer in this painting, which would be made in Paris. However, it was probably not until the regiment returned from Spain early in 1809 that it was possible to achieve this.

All the fittings of this officer's *schapska* are of silver lace or cord, or silvered metal. The blue centre of its French cockade is covered by a silver Maltese cross, a Polish national symbol commemorating the Confederation of Bar. The silver and crimson embroidery bordering all officers' *revers*, collars, cuffs and *retroussis* is uniquely Polish, consisting of three parallel silver cords with a fourth interwoven over and under the centre cord, all on a crimson background.

This officer's *banderole* of red morocco leather is covered with silver tissue and decorated with a silver shield, bearing a gold 'N', and a crowned gold eagle. Below his sash of silver thread, interwoven with crimson wool, he wears a sword-belt of red morocco leather, trimmed with silver braid. The rather plain steel scabbard makes a surprising contrast to the splendour of his attire. All metal fittings of his horse's harness are of silver, or have been silvered.

Garde Impériale - Chevau légers Polonais 1807-1814.

Officier supérieur. Tenue de grande parade.

PLATE 73

Garde Impériale – Chevau-légers Polonais. 1807–1814
Junior officer. Service full dress.

This young officer, perhaps a *lieutenant en premier* and, as such, a company commander, seems to be riding at the head of his squadron alongside its commander.

Every day of the year, whatever the circumstances, the uniform appropriate for the day's activities would be prescribed by the regiment's colonel and entered in the orders book of each company's *fourrier*. *Grande tenue de service*, a step down from *grande tenue*, might be ordered on the eve of a regiment's departure on campaign for a final inspection by the Emperor. Such luxurious elements of officers' uniforms and equipage as their white dress *kurtkas*, ball dress and dress schabraques would be packed away at the regimental depot. The regimental *ordonnances* were responsible for ensuring that their officers' extra uniforms and other necessities were placed in the assigned baggage wagons. Wealthier officers might be accompanied on campaign by a veritable household of their own.

The regiment of *Chevau-légers* became a regiment of *Chevau-légers lanciers* in an unusual manner. On 6 July 1809, in the final phase of the Battle of Wagram, the regiment was called on by Marshal MacDonald to drive off Austrian uhlans, who were pressing his corps hard. Struck by a furious Polish charge, the uhlans broke and fled, discarding their lances. The Poles picked up many of these and used them to good effect against Schwartzenberg's cavalry, which had come to the uhlans' aid.

After the battle, when the regiment's colonel, General Count Vincent Krasinski, asked Napoleon's permission to arm his men with lances, a traditional Polish weapon, the Emperor replied, 'Since they know so well how to use them, let them keep them!'

Garde Impériale ~ Chevau-légers Polonais. 1807-1814.

Officier subalterne. Grande tenue de service.

PLATE 74

Garde Impériale – Chevau-légers Polonais. 1807–1814
Kettledrummer.

This magnificent regimental *timbalier* was first depicted by Martinet in 1811, the kettledrummer having made his first public appearance during Napoleon's birthday celebrations on 15 August 1810.

The drummer was Louis Robiquet, a native of Lille, who had joined the regiment as a trumpeter in 1808. He had been appointed *timbalier* on I July 1810. After having served in the campaigns of Spain in 1808, and Germany in 1809, he went to Russia with the regiment and disappeared at Borisov during the retreat. There is no record of another regimental *timbalier* having been appointed.

Over a long-sleeved crimson waistcoat, the drummer wears a white tunic with false sleeves that hang down his back. His loose sky-blue trousers are tucked into fawn-coloured boots. His Polish-style hat is a *konfederatka*, with a fur turban surmounted by a band of gold lace set with semi-precious stones, jade or turquoise. The 'channels' of the hat's *pavillon* are stitched with gold thread, and its cords and flounders are of gold cord. Topping this magnificent structure are voluminous crimson and white plumes.

The gilded scales of the horse's head harness are set with jade and turquoise stones. Its housing is of crimson velvet, embroidered and bordered with gold lace, as are both drum banners. On each banner, a silver *banderole*, above a gold eagle within a golden laurel wreath, bears the regiment's title. The four corners of each banner are decorated with embroidered Imperial crowns, linked by scrolls of palms interspersed with lictors' fasces. The background of each banner is set with eighty-eight silver stars.

Garde Impériale - Chevau-légers Polonais. 1807-1814.
Timbalier.

PLATE 75

Garde Impériale – Chevau-légers Polonais. 1807–1814
Brigadier-trompette and trumpeters. Full dress. 1809–1814.

Although the precise date of the transformation of the dress uniforms of the regiment's trumpeters is not known, this probably occurred early in 1810, in preparation for the festivities associated with the Emperor's marriage to the Archduchess Marie-Louise. The most obvious change was a reversal of the colours of the *kurtka* and the *pavillon* (cloth upper portion) of the *schapska*. (In this painting, Rousselot has indicated crimson stitching in the 'channels' of the *schapskas' pavillons*, although this detail is missing from his *Planche* No. 65.)

Other changes included the addition of a belt and a *banderole de giberne* of leather covered with crimson cloth, on which were sewn three parallel strips of silver lace, the cloth showing between them. All metal parts of the *banderole* and belt were brass. The appearance of the aiguillettes was improved by substituting crimson wool for the white wool used in the first version. The schabraque and portmanteau remained essentially the same.

The *brigadier-trompette* is distinguished from the other trumpeters solely by his single silver lace chevron. The trumpeters were furnished with longer parade trumpets, incorporating a ball-like shape in the tube, reminiscent of eighteenth-century designs.

A school for trumpeters was established at Chantilly in 1811, initially with sixteen students, all destined for assignment to the regiment's companies as circumstances required, and as they proved physically qualified. (The oldest was fifteen, and the youngest seven.)

Garde Impériale ✕ Chevau-légers Polonais 1807-1814.

Brigadier-trompette et trompettes-Grande tenue. 1809-1814.

J. Rousselot

PLATE 76

Garde Impériale – Chevau-légers Polonais. 1807–1814
Trumpet-major and trumpeters. Parade uniform. 1809–1814.

What a dazzling spectacle the *tête de colonne* of the regiment must have presented, when led by these extraordinarily uniformed trumpeters. In this painting, the faces of the magnificent trumpet banners (*tabliers*) are clearly displayed, while the design of the reverse side is partially visible, hanging from the trumpet-major's instrument, which rests on his thigh. Both faces of the *tabliers* were fringed with bullion of twisted silver wire and crimson wool, being embroidered with silver and gold thread, highlighted by spangles. The golden spread-eagle on the *tablier*'s face held in its talons a silver ribbon, bearing the legend '*Chevau-légers Polonais*'. On the reverse of the *tablier*, a golden crowned 'N' was set within a silver laurel wreath, surmounted by a silver ribbon inscribed '*Garde Impériale*'.

The trumpet-major in the foreground is distinguished from his trumpeters by the white plume on his *schapska* which indicates his membership of the regiment's *petit état-major* (small headquarters staff), his three silver grade chevrons, the double row of lace on his collar, and the predominance of silver thread in his aiguillettes and other cording. He wears a brass scabbard, in contrast to the steel scabbards of his men.

Although no other instrumentalists were noted on the regiment's rolls, at times as many as ten trumpeters acted as trombonists and French horn players, led by a *maréchal-des-logis*. Apparently their preoccupation with such instruments was at the expense of their trumpet playing, since in 1810 the regiment's Major Dautancourt ordered that all instruments other than trumpets be taken away from them. One trumpeter, however, deserted, taking a trombone with him!

Many years after having completed this painting, Rousselot commented that he had made the trumpeters' *schapskas* too narrow. Only a perfectionist could detect such a subtle inaccuracy.

Garde Impériale - Chevau-légers Polonais. 1807-1814.

Trompette-major et trompettes - tenue de parade

1809 - 1814.

L. Rousselot

PLATE 77

Garde Impériale – Chevau-légers Polonais. 1807–1814
Officer eagle-bearer and troop, full dress in cloaks.

When the regiment was formed, the decree establishing its composition called for four eagle-bearers, but Napoleon reduced the number to one. A lieutenant was appointed to this position in 1807, being succeeded by another in 1810, although it was not until 30 June 1811 that the Emperor presented an eagle and standard to the regiment. Of gilded bronze, the eagle had on the front and back of its *caisson* (base) the number '1'. (With the establishment of the Second Regiment of Light Horse Lancers of the Guard in September 1810, the Polish Lancers had become the *1er Régiment de Chevau-légers-lanciers de la Garde Impériale*.) The standard was the 1804 model, bearing on its obverse the inscription, '*GARDE IMPÉRIALE L'EMPEREUR DES FRANÇAIS AU 1er RÉGIMENT DE CHEVAU-LÉGERS LANCIERS*'. On the reverse was a crowned spread-eagle and the inscription, '*VALEUR ET DISCIPLINE 1er ESCADRON*'.

That standard was not taken to Russia, but was left in the *grand salon* of the Tuileries, finally disappearing when the Empire died. In 1813, the regiment was given an 1812 model standard for its original eagle. The inscription on its obverse read, '*GARDE IMPÉRIALE L'EMPEREUR NAPOLÉON AU 1er RÉGIMENT DE CHEVAU-LÉGERS LANCIERS*'. Nothing is known of any inscriptions on its reverse, although there may have been the names of battles and capitals entered. That eagle and standard did not accompany the regiment during the 1813 and 1814 campaigns, although the final *porte-aigle*, Rostworowski, was wounded at Reichenbach in 1813. It seems probable, however, that the regiment had with it at least a colonel's *fanion*, since such a standard, in the form of a two-pointed lance pennon, exists in a Warsaw museum.

Although Rousselot uses the simple term *manteau* (cloak) here, the men are actually wearing the *manteau capote* (caped overcoat) adopted in 1813.

J. Roussalat

Garde Impériale ~ Chevau-légers Polonais. 1807-1814.

Officier porte-aigle et troupe, grande tenue en manteau.

PLATE 78

Garde Impériale – Chevau-légers Polonais. 1807–1814
Parade uniform after 1809.

In this painting, Rousselot presents the image most often associated with the troopers of this regiment. The reason for the scene being 'after 1809' is because it was in that year that the regiment added the lance to its troopers' already formidable armament of two pistols, a carbine and a sabre. The steel head of the lance was attached by two bands of steel that extended down the shaft and were screwed to it. The crimson and white *flamme* was attached to one of those bands by three screws. Taffeta *flammes* were provided for dress occasions, and serge for general service.

At this time, the regiment was still attempting to establish uniformity in its armament by gradually disposing of the 'hand-me-down' assortment of Prussian pistols and muskets with which it had begun its service.

For this occasion, the troopers have left their carbines at the regimental depot in Chantilly. Plate 90 shows how they were carried once the lance occupied the rider's right hand and side. It is noteworthy, however, that a socket for the end of the lance is attached to the trooper's left stirrup, presumably in case he needs to shift the lance to his left for an extended period.

Parade dress requires the addition of the plume and white cords and flounders to the troopers' *schapskas*. Their cloaks will have been left in the barracks on this occasion, rather than being strapped beneath their portmanteaus.

L. Rousselot

Garde Impériale - Chevau-légers Polonais 1807-1814.

Tenue de parade après 1809.

PLATE 79

Garde Impériale – Chevau-légers Polonais. 1807–1814
Trumpeter, service full dress, and *Fourrier*.

There is no evidence that initially there was a second uniform for the trumpeters. Consequently, they took part in the campaigns of 1808 in Spain, and 1809 in Austria, in their crimson *kurtkas*. It was probably only when the white *kurtkas* were introduced, early in 1810, that sky-blue *kurtkas* and trousers were furnished to the trumpeters as a service uniform. Prior to 1810, they had been utilising the schabraques of the troops for service dress, and they continued to do so.

A trumpeter would wear his *grande tenue de service*, for example, when he was a member of the duty squadron assigned to the Emperor in the field. In this uniform, his *schapska*, its cords and plume, and his aiguillettes and epaulettes would be those of his dress uniform, but his *porte-giberne*, the *giberne* itself, his *ceinturon* (belt), his sword-belt and straps, and his sword-knot would be those of the troop. His 'parade' trumpet would have been exchanged for a less elaborate instrument.

The *fourrier*'s uniform is differentiated from that of the troop by a silver lace chevron above each cuff of his *kurtka*, a single row of silver lace on his collar, the silver braid stripe of his grade on each upper sleeve, and the third silver/two-thirds crimson thread mixture of his aiguillettes and *schapska* cords and flounders.

Garde Impériale ~ Chevau-légers Polonais 1807-1814

Trompette, grande tenue de service, et Fourrier.

L. Rousselot

PLATE 80

Garde Impériale – Chevau-légers Polonais. 1807–1814
Officer in undress *kurtka*. Trumpeter, *brigadier* and troopers in guard dress.

The uniform of the trumpeter shown here is essentially identical to that in the previous painting, differing only in the absence of the *schapska*'s plume and cords.

The collar and cuffs of the *brigadier*'s *kurtka* are decorated with single rows of silver lace, indicating his rank, but his epaulettes and aiguillettes are those of the troop, since he is not an NCO. The stitched edging of the men's buff leather belts, clearly visible here, was a distinction peculiar to the Guard.

The officer's *petite tenue kurtka* differs from his dress *kurtka* in that it has dark blue *revers* with crimson piping, rather than crimson, lace-bordered *revers*. However, it retains the lace trim on the cuffs, collar and *retroussis*. His trousers are of the same design as his dress trousers, but probably of poorer quality. Their gaiter-like fit over his insteps is clearly evident.

The officer's sword-belt of red morocco leather, closed by a buckle of silver hooks, is trimmed with silver lace. His chasseur-style sabre is derived from the light cavalry model of the Year XI. His dress *banderole* is protected by a leather sheath, closed with silver buttons. He has covered his *schapska* with a translucent oiled silk cover, and, for convenience while reading the guard's orders, he has suspended the end of its linked silver chain chin-strap from a hook on the right-hand corner of the *schapska*'s *pavillon*.

Garde Impériale ~ Chevau-légers Polonais 1807-1814.

Officier en kurtka de petite tenue.

Trompette, Brigadier et Chevau-légers en tenue de garde.

PLATE 81

Garde Impériale – Chevau-légers Polonais. 1807–1814
Master workman in walking-out dress and trooper in stable dress.

The *maître-ouvrier* seen in this painting seems to be the regiment's master tailor. As such, he is one of a number of specialists who attend to the day-to-day uniform and equipment needs of the regiment. These include a master trouser-maker, a master boot-maker, a master armourer, a master saddler, a master spur-maker and a sergeant farrier.

As an NCO, the master tailor's walking-out dress is generally similar to that of the regiment's officers. The *habit* has silver-lace-trimmed, dark blue *revers* coming to points, its crimson collar edged with silver lace, and its dark blue *retroussis* piped in crimson and possibly decorated with crowned Imperial eagles embroidered in white thread. His crimson waistcoat is trimmed with the mixed silver and crimson braid of NCOs, as are his Hungarian-style breeches. The tops of his Souvorov-style boots are edged with the same braid. His *chapeau* is ornamented by a white plume, a simple French cockade held in place by a silver lace strap, and crimson and silver thread tufts in each corner. (As a Frenchman, the tailor has omitted the Maltese cross from the cockade on his *chapeau*.)

The *chevau-léger*'s stable dress comprises his *bonnet de police*, a plain blue stable jacket and his *pantalon de voyage*. The trousers held by the trooper clearly display the unusual manner for ensuring their snug fit.

Garde Impériale - Chevau-légers Polonais 1807-1814.

Maître-ouvrier en tenue de ville et chevau-léger en tenue d'écurie.

PLATE 82

Garde Impériale – Chevau-légers Polonais. 1807–1814
Maréchal-des-logis and *Maréchal-des-logis-chef*; Sunday walking-out dress.

It is hardly surprising that the brilliant uniforms of these two non-commissioned officers have attracted some feminine companions during a Sunday outing. Although NCOs, such as the *maître-ouvrier* in the previous painting, could obtain, at their own expense, *habits* and *redingotes* for off-duty wear, this scene takes place on a Sunday during a season when dress uniforms, with sabres, are prescribed by regulations for walking-out in town.

The *maréchal-des-logis-chef*'s uniform differs in two respects from that of his comrade: he has a third silver lace grade chevron on each sleeve; and the proportion of silver thread to crimson silk in his aiguillettes is two to one, as opposed to one to two. (That was true for *all* NCOs until 1811.) In the cords and flounders decorating their *schapskas*, the crimson silk dominates. The seam joining the *pavillon* of an NCO's *schapska* to its black leather lower portion is covered with silver lace, in contrast to the white thread braid of the trooper's *schapska*.

Because officers and troopers of the regiment almost always wore full-length trousers, unlike the men of the other three elite Guard cavalry regiments, they had little need for any boots other than the low-cut type issued to them. These fitted easily beneath their tight trousers.

Garde Impériale ~ Chevau-légers Polonais. 1807-1814.

Maréchal des Logis et Maréchal des Logis-Chef: Tenue de sortie du dimanche.

Plate 83

Garde Impériale – Chevau-légers Polonais. 1807–1814
Light-horseman and trumpeter in weekday walking-out dress.

Observing these two young soldiers enjoying a glass of *vin rouge*, perhaps in one of the charming little bars in Grinzing, on the hills above Vienna, allows us to appreciate the most obvious difference between their service uniforms and the weekday walking-out dress, which they are wearing. Both have turned under the crimson, lace-trimmed *revers* of their *kurtkas* to spare them unnecessary wear. The undecorated *revers* thus exposed are dark blue in one case, sky-blue in the other, both being piped in crimson.

The fact that the men are wearing their aiguillettes on their left shoulders signifies that the scene takes place some time after the Battle of Wagram, in 1809, which led to the regiment being provided with lances. (Aiguillettes and a lance on the same side of a trooper could be a troublesome combination.)

For weekday outings, both men wear their *schapskas* without plumes, dress cords or flounders. Their trousers are of the same cut and design as those worn with service dress or their parade uniforms, although each has probably reserved an especially fine pair for the latter occasions.

The crimson-piped cloth tab on the left side of the *kurtka* ensures that the waist-belt will not ride up or down. The men wear their sword-belts beneath their *kurtkas*.

L. Rousselet

Garde Impériale – Chevau-légers Polonais 1807-1814.

Chevau-léger et trompette en tenue de ville de semaine.

PLATE 84

Garde Impériale – Chevau-légers Polonais. 1807–1814
Officers in society and quarters dress.

The officer on the left in this painting is wearing a relatively simple *habit*, ornamented only by crimson and silver lace on its collar and cuffs. Its dark blue *revers en pointe* are piped in crimson, and its *retroussis* are dark blue, piped with crimson, but without other ornamentation. The collar points of his white dress shirt appear above his black silk stock.

He has attached a white plume to his hat, which is decorated with a large cockade beneath a strap of silver lace and two silver cords on each wing. From its ends emerge tassels of twisted silver thread. A plain white waistcoat, breeches, stockings and silver-buckled shoes complete his costume. He is wearing a sword-belt, but does not appear to have hung from it his dress épée.

The quarters dress of his older colleague, perhaps the regimental adjutant-major, consists of his *surtout*, beneath which he wears a white waistcoat, and his uniform trousers. On his breast is the ribbon of the Legion. His undress hat, on the table, is a *konfederatka* of supple crimson cloth. Its crimson band, decorated with lace of embroidered silver oak and laurel leaves, indicates his senior rank.

Garde Impériale ~ Chevau-légers Polonais. 1807-1814.

Officiers en tenue de société et en tenue de quartier.

PLATE 85

Garde Impériale – Chevau-légers Polonais. 1807–1814
Officers in ball dress.

If the gold-encrusted blue coat on the far side of the fireplace is that of a marshal, his presence does not seem to be inhibiting these smartly turned out young officers and their charming acquaintances. For this occasion, both officers have donned white *habits*, with crimson *revers*, collars and cuffs, all trimmed with crimson and silver lace. Although Rousselot's *Planche* No. 75 illustrates such a coat with very elaborate arrow-like silver buttonhole decorations on its *revers* and similar embroidery on its collar, he notes that these details were based on a miniature of an individual officer. The artist's failure to incorporate them in this painting suggests that he considered the design not to have been the norm.

The officers' white silk waistcoats, decorated with silver brandenburgs and buttons, add to the splendour of their attire. The silver buttons, sewn to the point at which the corners of the *retroussis* of the *habit*'s tails meet, are noteworthy. Both officers are wearing their dress épées.

The artist's great skill in conveying the candle-lit gaiety pervading this handsome apartment helps carry us back in time, when the brilliance of such social occasions and the risk of fatal encounters on the battle-field might be no more than hours apart.

Garde Impériale ~ Chevau-légers Polonais 1807-1814.
Officiers en tenue de bal.

PLATE 86

Garde Impériale – Chevau-légers Polonais. 1807–1814
Officer in campaign dress.

Some of the glitter and panache of this officer's dress uniform has been put away for the duration of the campaign – at least, until the prospect of a battle looms, when it will quickly reappear – but other elements of it remain unchanged.

The plume and silver cords and flounders of his *schapska* have been stowed away in his portmanteau, while the hat itself has been encased in a translucent oiled cloth cover. His crimson *revers* have been turned under, being buttoned toward his aiguillettes. He has left the top of the *revers* unbuttoned and slightly turned back, perhaps to make it easier to reach an inside pocket. His *banderole* and the glistening gold and silver cover of his *giberne* have been provided with leather cases, the former fastened with silver buttons. His dress *ceinturon* has been replaced by a plain white buff leather belt.

The trousers he wears are those of his service and dress uniforms, however, as are his schabraque and portmanteau, although all are probably 'second-best'. His horse's harness is less richly decorated with silver ornamentation than the dress version, and the woven silver parade bridle has been replaced by one of black leather.

The troopers in the background have also turned under their *revers*, covered their *schapskas* and removed the *flammes* from their lances.

L. Rousselot

Garde Impériale - Chevau-légers Polonais 1807-1814
Officier en tenue de campagne.

PLATE 87

Garde Impériale – Chevau-légers Polonais. 1807–1814
Officer on campaign. 1812.

With this painting, Rousselot shows an early stage of the fateful Russian campaign. The dress of this officer differs from that of the officer in the previous painting in only two respects. He has donned looser trousers more suited to rough field conditions – such as fording streams. They are reinforced with leather panels on the inside of each leg and around their bottoms. He is also wearing his undress *giberne*, rather than its luxurious gold- and silver-plated dress counterpart.

He and his men are performing outpost duty ahead of the massive French Army as it makes its ponderous way eastward, a type of duty that the *Chevau-légers* first learned under the tutelage of General Lasalle in Spain. The fact that the officer has unsheathed his sabre suggests that he anticipates possible contact with cossacks screening Barclay de Tolly's withdrawing Russian Army.

Arriving in the vicinity of Vilna at the River Vilia, where the Russians had destroyed the bridges, Napoleon ordered the service squadron, the first squadron of the *Chevau-légers*, to swim the river. Led by *Chef d'escadron* Kozietulski, the horsemen plunged into the river with cries of 'Vive l'Empereur!' When it became evident that the force of the current was such that some of the men were in danger of drowning, General Krasinski and several officers who were good swimmers threw themselves into the river to save their men. Thus the loss to the regiment was limited to one trooper.

L. Rousselot

Garde Impériale ~ Chevau-légers Polonais. 1807-1814.

Officier en campagne. 1812.

PLATE 88

Garde Impériale – Chevau-légers Polonais. 1807–1814
Trumpeter in campaign dress.

This painting may be taken to indicate that the French forces have moved another stage closer to their final goal of Moscow, and are approaching Smolensk. The scene shows a skirmish between men of what is now the *1er Régiment de Chevau-légers lanciers* and Russian dragoons of the Pskov Regiment.

At dawn on 17 October, the regiment had encountered some 200 Russian cavalrymen on a plateau on the right bank of the Dniepr. They charged them, intending to corner and capture them at the riverside. However, as they drove the Russians toward the river, the Polish squadrons came under the fire of Russian infantry and artillery disposed along the right bank, and *Chef d'escadron* Kozietulski was severely wounded. The arrival of the Second Regiment of Guard Lancers, and the deployment of French artillery by General Montbrun, redressed the situation, however, and the Russians were forced to conduct a fighting withdrawal over the river.

Having sounded the charge, our trumpeter has tossed his instrument over his shoulder and is demonstrating that he is every bit a fighting member of the regiment. Like his comrades, he wears his *pantalon de voyage*, has turned under the crimson *revers* of his *kurtka*, and encased his *schapska* in its protective cover. The men have been travelling with the points of their schabraques hooked up to avoid soiling them and have hung sacks of oats from the cantles of their saddles. Up to this point, through their familiarity with the terrain and general conditions, the Poles had managed somewhat better than other cavalry regiments to keep their mounts in good condition.

L. Rousselot

Garde Impériale - Chevau-légers Polonais 1807-1814.

Trompette en tenue de campagne.

PLATE 89

Garde Impériale – Chevau-légers Polonais. 1807–1814
Campaign dress in cloaks.

It scarcely requires great powers of imagination to associate this bleak scene with the retreat of the remnants of the *Grande Armée* from Moscow. While the *Chevau-légers* were more accustomed to the harsh conditions than many of the other surviving troops, after the battle at Krasnoye on 17 November, the strength of the regiment was down to 340, of whom only a third were still mounted. As required, the latter made up the service squadron.

When the Emperor and Guard reached Smorgoni on 5 December, about a hundred well-mounted reinforcements from the depot at Königsberg were awaiting the regiment. With Napoleon when he left the army that evening was an escort of troopers from the Guard Chasseurs and the *Chevau-légers*. After Ozmiana, the Chasseurs had been so reduced in number that escort duties were taken over entirely by the *Chevau-légers* and troopers from the 7th Polish lancer regiment. By the time Napoleon reached the relay station at Rovnopol, two-thirds of his escort had died from the cold along the way. At that point, Neapolitan horse took over the escort duty.

At Vilna on 10 December, the regiment could still muster 432 men, but only 185 of them had been among the 1109 who had crossed the Niemen little more than four months previously.

The fact that the three *Chevau-légers* in this painting have pennons attached to their lances, even in this desolate landscape, suggests that they may be part of the Emperor's escort. There can be little question, however, as to the source of the meat that the trooper is attempting to cook on the end of his carbine's ramrod.

Garde Impériale » Chevau-légers Polonais 1807-1814.

Tenue de campagne en manteau.

PLATE 90

Garde Impériale – Chevau-légers Polonais. 1807–1814
Campaign dress 1812–1813.

In this painting, we can see how carbines were carried as a consequence of the *Chevau-légers'* adopting the lance. However, when the regiment was reorganised in April 1813, a major change was made in the troopers' armament to adapt it more closely to combat circumstances, since it had become evident that the second rank in a charge didn't need lances. The change also had the benefit of reducing the total weight carried by each trooper and his mount. From then on, the battle formation of a company of 125 troopers was as set out below.

First rank: two *maréchaux-des-logis*, each with sabre and two pistols; four *brigadiers*, each with sabre, carbine, bayonet, pistol and lance; forty-four *cavaliers*, each with sabre, pistol and lance. Second rank: four *brigadiers* and forty-four *cavaliers*, all with sabre, pistol, carbine and bayonet. In addition to those four platoons: three *trompettes*, each with sabre and two pistols; two *maréchaux-ferrants*, each with sabre and pistol; nine *lanciers*, armed as first-rank *cavaliers*; nine *carabiniers*, armed as second-rank *cavaliers*. Behind the second rank were one *maréchal-des-logis-chef*, two *maréchaux-des-logis* and a *fourrier*, all with sabre and two pistols.

This resulted in some changes of equipment. The *porte-mousqueton, porte-baionnette* and the carbine boot were taken away from the lancers, while the lance boot was removed from the *carabiniers*. Only the four *brigadiers* of the first rank kept the full allowance of arms.

Garde Impériale - Chevau-légers Polonais 1807-1814.

Tenue de campagne 1812-1813.

Plate 91

Garde Impériale – Chevau-légers Polonais. 1807–1814
Campaign dress. 1814.

It was common practice at that time for armies to prepare for a major battle by donning dress uniforms. In the case of the *Chevau-légers*, this meant opening their crimson *revers*, uncovering and decorating their *schapskas*, changing into their service trousers and unhooking the points of their schabraques. However, during the three desperate months of the Campaign of France, there was little time for such niceties. As Napoleon struggled to thwart the advance of the Coalition armies on Paris, his tactics put his constantly dwindling forces to the most gruelling of physical and psychological tests, yet they emerged with unbroken spirit.

Rousselot has portrayed these Lancers in the costume they were to wear constantly throughout those months. The *pantalon de voyage* are a slight variation of those with which we are already familiar. Perhaps the side-buttoning trousers had proved to be more trouble than they were worth.

The *Chevau-légers* distinguished themselves in every battle of the campaign: Brienne, Montmirail, Vauchamps, Montereau, Berry-au-Bac, Craonne and Rheims. Finally, after the fall of Paris, General Krasinski led the regiment to Fontainebleau. With Napoleon's abdication, the decision was taken to return the regiment to Poland. When Krasinski asked for volunteers from the assembled Polish forces to join the guard of 400 soldiers who were to accompany Napoleon to Elba, 6000 men stepped forward. Krasinski personally selected 109 lancers of the *Chevau-légers*, and Major Paul Jerzmanowski – who would be wounded at Waterloo a year later – was given the honour of commanding them. The remainder of the regiment would return to Poland and offer their services to the victorious Alexander.

Garde Impériale ~ Chevau-légers Polonais. 1807-1814.

Tenue de Campagne . 1814.

L. Rousselot

APPENDIX I
Senior Officers of the Guard Cavalry

Overall Guard

Bessières, Marshal Jean-Baptiste, 1768–1813.
Chef d'escadron 1797; *Colonel commandant des Guides* 1798; commander of the Guard of the *Corps legislatif* 1799; *général de brigade* 1800; commander of the Consular Guard 1801; *général de division* 1802; commander of the Imperial Guard 1804; *Maréchal de l'Empire* 1804; *Duc d'Istrie* 1809; commander of the Guard, Paris, 1810, Spain, 1811; commanded the Guard cavalry in Russian campaign; killed at Rippach, Saxony, 1 May 1813.

Nansouty, General Count Étienne Marie Antoine Champion, 1768–1815.
Général de brigade 1799; *général de division* 1803; wounded at Borodino; commanded the Guard cavalry, as *colonel-général* of the Dragoons, July 1813; during first Restoration, aide to the Comte d'Artois, and Captain-lieutenant of the Grey Musketeers; died in Paris, 12 February 1815.

Sébastiani, General Count Horace François Bastien de la Porta, 1772–1851.
Général de brigade 1803; *général de division* 1805; wounded at Austerlitz; sent to Turkey as ambassador, 1806, where he organised the defence of Constantinople against a British attack; wounded at Leipzig; replaced Nansouty as commander of the Guard cavalry, 1814, after Craonne; rejoined Napoleon, 1815, in a National Guard command; Marshal of France 1840.

Grenadiers à cheval

Castex, Major-general Baron Bertrand-Pierre. 1771–1842.
Commander of Young Guard Horse Grenadiers 1813; commanded Guard cavalry of Northern Army 1814; retired 1814.

Guindey, Assistant Adjutant-major.
During Jena campaign, as *maréchal-des-logis* of 10th Hussars, killed Prince Louis of Prussia at Saalfield; killed at Hanau.

Laferrière-Lévêque, Count.
Général de brigade 1811; *commander en second* of regiment 1813; succeeded Lepic as commander of Horse Grenadiers; lost a leg at Craonne, 7 March 1814; commandant of the cavalry school at Saumur during first Restoration.

Lepic, General Count Louis, 1765–1825.
Lieutenant-colonel of Grenadiers 1805; *colonel-major, commandant en second,* at Eylau, where he was wounded; *général de brigade* 1807; commanded Guard detachment in Spain 1808; commander of Horse Guard in Spain 1810; *général de division* 1813; colonel of 2nd *Gardes d'Honneur* 1813.

Ordener, General Count Michel, 1755–1811.
Commandant of Horse Grenadiers of Consular Guard, July 1800; *général de brigade* 1804; *général de division* 1805; commander of Guard cavalry, 1805; seriously wounded at Austerlitz; retired from active service, May 1806.

Remy, Baron.
Squadron commander of Grenadiers in Spain 1810.

Walther, General Count Frédéric Henri, 1761–1813.
Général de brigade 1793; *général de division* 1803; wounded at Austerlitz, as commander of 2nd dragoon division; replaced Ordener as commander of Horse Grenadiers, 20 May 1806; commander of Guard cavalry at Wagram; Russian campaign; continued as commander of Horse Grenadiers 1813; led 3rd Guard cavalry division at Leipzig; last battle at Hanau 1813; died 24 November 1813.

Chasseurs à cheval

Beauharnais, Prince Eugène de, 1781–1824.
Captain of Chasseurs, Consular Guard 1799; *chef d'escadron* 1800; *colonel-général* of Chasseurs 1804; Viceroy of Italy, 13 May 1805; nominal commander of Chasseurs until 1809.

Dahlmann, General Nicolas, 1769–1807.
Guides de Bonaparte; chef d'escadron, Chasseurs 1802; general adjutant of Consular Guard; commander of Chasseurs after death of Morland at Austerlitz, December 1805; *général de brigade* 1806; killed at Eylau 1807.

Daumesnil, General Baron Pierre, 1777–1832.
Guides 1797; lieutenant of Chasseurs 1800; *chef d'escadron* 1805; promoted to major after Austerlitz; wounded at Madrid; under Guyot in Chasseurs at Wagram, where he lost a leg; commandant of Château de Vincennes 1814, 1815 and 1830.

Delaître, General Baron Antoine Charles Bernard, 1776–1838.
Quartermaster, Mameluks, Consular Guard; major 1805; transferred to Polish Light Horse as one of regiment's two majors, April 1807; lieutenant-colonel 1808; commanded Guard light cavalry regiment 1810.

Desmichels, General Baron.
As captain, awarded Star of the Legion for capture of Austrian dragoons after Ulm; major of Chasseurs 1807, wounded at Eylau; general 1814.

Exelmans, General Count Rémy-Joseph-Isidore, 1775–1852.
Général de brigade 1807; *colonel-major* of Chasseurs 1811; *général de division* 1812; commanded 2nd division of Guard cavalry 1814; led 2nd cavalry corps at Waterloo; as supporter of Louis Napoleon, made Marshal of France 1851.

Guyot, General Count Claude-Étienne, 1768–1837.
Captain of Chasseurs in Consular Guard 1802; *colonel en second* Chasseurs, December 1805; commander of Chasseurs in Spain after capture of Lefèbvre-Desnouëttes; commander of Guard light cavalry at Wagram, 6 July 1809; *général de brigade* 1809; commander of Napoleon's escort to Spain; in absence of Lefèbvre-Desnouëttes, commanded Chasseurs 1811; *commandant en second* 1813; wounded at Lützen and captured at Kulm, but quickly exchanged; commander of Guard heavy cavalry 1814; commander of *Corps Royal des Cuirassiers de France* (former Guard Horse Grenadiers) during first Restoration; commander of Guard heavy cavalry at Ligny and Waterloo 1815; recalled to the army by Louis-Philippe.

Kirmann, Chevalier.
Chef d'escadron Spain 1810; commanded Mameluks in Russia; commander of Mameluks 1813; *chef d'escadron* of Chasseurs at Saint-Dizier 1814; during first Restoration, remained as Chasseur *chef d'escadron*; with Chasseurs during Waterloo campaign and until regiment's dissolution.

Lefèbvre-Desnouëttes, General Count Charles, 1773–1822.
Aide de camp of the First Consul 1800; colonel of the 18th dragoons 1802; *général de brigade* of Bavarian cavalry 1806; *général de division*, aide de camp to Prince Jérôme of Westphalia 1807; *colonel-major* of Chasseurs and Mameluks, January 1808; wounded at Saragossa 1808; *général de division* 1808; wounded and captured by British at Benavente 1808; left England by violating parole 1811; commanded division of Old Guard cavalry in Russia; wounded at Vinhovo; commanded light cavalry division of Guard 1813 and 1814; wounded twice at Brienne; commanded *Corps Royal des Chasseurs à cheval de France* during the first Restoration; commanded light cavalry of Guard during Waterloo campaign; wounded at Waterloo; proscribed by the monarchy, went to the United States, but was drowned while returning to France.

Lion, General Count Jean, 1765–1825.
Colonel-major of Chasseurs 1809; *commandant en second* to Guyot in Spain; *général de brigade*, commander of Guard cavalry, February 1813; commanded Old Guard squadrons in 3rd division 1813; wounded at Vauchamps; *général de division* 1815; vice commander of *Corps Royal des Chasseurs à cheval de France* 1814; rallied to Napoleon; commanded regiment at its dissolution in 1815.

Meuziau, General Baron.
Général de brigade, *colonel-major* of Chasseur Young Guard squadrons 1813; inspector of cavalry during the first Restoration; recalled to the army by Louis-Philippe.

Morland, Colonel François de, 1771–1805.
Chef d'escadron of Chasseurs 1802; *colonel commandant en second* under de Beauharnais 1805; effective commander of Chasseurs 1805; killed at Austerlitz, December 1805.

Dragons de l'Impératrice

Arrighi de Casanova, General Jean-Toussaint, Duke of Padua, 1778–1853.
First commander of the Dragoons; *général de brigade* 1807; in Spain 1809; took command of corps of cuirassiers after death of d'Espagne; took part in the Campaign of France 1814; forced into retirement during first Restoration; Governor of *les Invalides* 1852.

Letort, General Baron Louis-Michel, 1773–1815.
Colonel 14th dragoons 1806; lieutenant-colonel of Guard Dragoons; in Spain with dragoons, returning with regiment for Essling, May 1809; *général de brigade*, vice commander of regiment in Russia 1812; *colonel-major*, one of two regimental commandants, 1813; *général de division*, commander of Young Guard squadrons in 3rd Division under Walther 1814; Château-Thierry 1814; earned a third Star of the Legion from Napoleon; vice-commander under Ornano of *Dragons de France* during first Restoration; commanded Dragoons May 1815; mortally wounded at Fleurus, 16 June 1815.

Marthod, Lieutenant-colonel.
Commanded Guard heavy cavalry detachment in Spain; killed at Bezovska 1812.

Ornano, General Count Philippe-Antoine, 1784–1863.
Cousin of Napoleon; colonel of 25th Dragoons 1807; *général de brigade* 1811; *général de division* 1812; although seriously wounded and left for dead on the battlefield of Krasnoye in 1812, he recovered; given responsibility for reconstituting the Guard Dragoons as their *colonel-major* 1813; commanded the heavy division of Guard cavalry 1813; commander of the *Dragons de France* during the first Restoration; missed Waterloo because of a wound from a duel; died as a Marshal of France and Governor of *les Invalides*.

Pinteville, Lieutenant-colonel.
Commanded Young Guard Dragoons of 1st Division, August 1813; retired from wounds 1814.

Saint-Sulpice, General Count Raymond-Gaspard de Bonardi, 1761–1835.
Général de brigade 1803; *général de division* and wounded at Eylau 1807; replaced Arrighi as commander of Dragoons, 6 June 1809; commanded Guard cavalry division in Russia; replaced by Ornano, 21 January 1813; became Governor of Fontainebleau; colonel of 4th *Gardes d'Honneur* 1813; retired 1815.

Testot-Ferry, Lieutenant-colonel.
Major of Dragoons, made commandant of Scout-Grenadiers, January 1814; made Baron for actions at Craonne.

Chevau-légers Polonais

Chlapowski, General Baron Dezydery, 1790–1879.
Awarded *Légion d'Honneur*, March 1807; orderly officer to Napoleon in Spain 1808; *chef d'escadron* of regiment, 13 January 1811; served with distinction in Russia; commanded two squadrons during 1813 campaign; distinguished himself at Reichenbach; left French service, July 1813.

Dautancourt, General Baron.
Joined *Chevau-légers* as lieutenant-colonel of *Gendarmerie d'Élite* when regiment established; cavalry commander in Russia; commanded Old Guard companies assigned to Emperor's escort 1813; promoted to general after Hanau; commander of Guard cavalry 1814; distinguished himself with Dragoons at Montmirail; commanded Guard cavalry in defence of Paris; commander of Elite Gendarmes, April 1815; recalled to the army by Louis-Philippe.

Dobieski, *Chef d'escadron* Vincent.
Already a holder of *Légion d'Honneur*, given a battlefield promotion and a second Star by Napoleon for actions at Château-Thierry.

Fredro, *Chef d'escadron* Severin.
Awarded *Légion d'Honneur*, August 1809; commander of Napoleon's escort from Oshmiany 1812.

Jankowski, *Chef d'escadron*.
Awarded Star of the Legion for capture of Colonel Blücher of Prussian hussars at Dresden 1813.

Jerzmanowski, Lieutenant-colonel Baron Paul.
Chef d'escadron in Russia; one of regimental majors 1813; led Polish Lancers to Elba; commanded first squadron of Light Horse, April 1815; in May, as *colonel-major*, given command of regiment of Light Horse Lancers, which he led at Waterloo, where he was wounded.

Kozietulski, Lieutenant-colonel.
Commander of Warsaw Guard of Honour during Napoleon's visit 1807; led 3rd Squadron in first attempt to open road at Somosierra, receiving eleven wounds; officer of the Legion 1809; wounded while saving Napoleon from cossacks after Malojaroslavets; *chef d'escadron* with 2nd Lancers 1813; commander of 1st Scout-Lancers, January 1814; led regiment during defence of Paris.

Krasinski, General Count Vincent Corvin, 1783–1876.
Colonel of lancers in Dombrowski's army; chosen by Napoleon as commander of newly formed *Chevau-légers Polonais*, with the rank of *colonel-major* 1807; *général de brigade* 1811; *général de division* 1813; commanded Young Guard cavalry brigade at Le Rothière, Montmirail and Rheims; commander-in-chief of Polish troops in France, April 1814; led the majority of troops back to Poland; wounded at Madrid, Wagram, Borodino and Arcis-sur-Aube.

Pac, General Count Louis Michel, 1778–1835.
Awarded *Légion d'Honneur* 1809; aide de camp to Napoleon 1812; led 900 *Chevau-légers Polonais* in Campaign of France 1814.

Zaluski, General Count Josef.
Participant in Russian and Saxony campaigns; disillusioned by Napoleon's abandonment of the concept of a free Poland; asked to be released from French service 1813.

APPENDIX II
Other Cavalry Regiments and Units of the Guard

Mameluks
Formed 13 October 1801. In 1814, seven Mameluks went with Napoleon to Elba. Other Old Guard Mameluks were incorporated in the *Corps Royal de Chasseurs de France*, while the Young Guard Mameluks became part of the Seventh Chasseurs. An Imperial decree, of 24 April 1815, ordered the reconstitution of a squadron of Mameluks, to be attached to the Chasseurs of the Guard.

Gendarmerie d'Élite
Formed on 19 March 1802, the *Gendarmerie d'Élite* was disbanded in 1814. However, some of its members were absorbed into the *Gendarmerie des Voyages et Chasses du Roi* during the first Restoration. The Elite Gendarmes were reformed on 8 April 1815.

Lanciers de Berg
This regiment was admitted to the Guard on 17 December 1809. A second regiment was formed in 1812, and in 1813, they were combined. Disbanded as unreliable after the Battle of Leipzig, some of its men entered Prussian service.

2ème Régiment de Chevau-légers lanciers
The 'Red Lancers' were formed in September 1810. In 1814, the Old Guard squadrons became the *Corps Royal des Chevau-légers lanciers de France*. The regiment was reformed in April 1815, but disbanded in September of that year.

Tartares Lithuaniens
This unit was formed on 24 August 1812, being incorporated in the Scout-Lancers in 1813.

3ème Régiment de Chevau-légers lanciers (Lithuanien)
Formed in 1812, this regiment was almost completely destroyed in Russia. In 1813, the survivors were placed in the 1st Regiment.

Gardes d'Honneur
The 1st to 4th regiments were established in April 1813, being disbanded in July 1814.

1er Régiment d'Eclaireurs
Created in December 1813, this unit was attached to the *Grenadiers à cheval*. It was disbanded in July 1814.

2ème Régiment d'Eclaireurs
Created in December 1813, this unit was attached to the *Dragons de l'Impératrice*. It was disbanded in 1814.

3ème Régiment d'Eclaireurs
Created in December 1813, this unit was attached to the *1er Chevau-légers lanciers*. It was also disbanded in 1814.

APPENDIX III
La Légion d'Honneur

A law of 19 May 1802 created the *Legion d'Honneur* as an award for both military bravery and civic accomplishment. However, it was not until 11 July 1804 that the design of the medal had been approved by Napoleon, allowing the first awards to be made.

Initially, four grades of the award were established: *légionnaire* (later *chevalier*), *officier*, *commandant* (later *commandeur*) and *grand officier*. In 1805, a fifth grade, *grand-aigle*, was established. The last award took the form of a medal that was suspended from the end of a crimson sash, or a large embroidered plaque worn on the left breast.

The original medal was a star (*étoile*) with five white-enamelled, double-pointed rays, although there were five later models during the life of the Empire. The centre of the star was silver for *chevaliers*, and gold for the other grades. On its obverse was the head of Napoleon, surrounded by the inscription, '*Napoléon Empereur des Français*'. The reverse bore an Imperial eagle holding thunderbolts, and the inscription, '*Honneur et Patrie*'. The ribbon for the stars of officers had a rosette in its centre.

Initially, it had been intended to limit the number of awards to 5500, but by 1815, 34,000 military and 1500 civilian awards had been made. When Louis XVIII regained the throne, the prestige that the Legion had acquired was such that the King chose not to abolish it, contenting himself with removing its Napoleonic associations.

BIBLIOGRAPHY

Brécard, General C.T., *L'Armée Française à Travers les Ages – La Cavalerie*, Paris, *Société des Editions Militaires*, 1931.

Brown, Anne S.K., *The Anatomy of Glory* (adapted from *Napoléon et la Garde Impériale*, by Henry Lachouque), Providence, Brown University Press, 1961. Reprinted Greenhill Books, London, 1997.

Bucquoy, Commandant E.L., *Les Uniformes du 1er Empire. La Garde Impériale – Troupes à cheval*, Paris, Jacques Grancher, 1977.

Chandler, David, *The Campaigns of Napoleon*, New York, Macmillan Company, 1966.

Charrié, Pierre, *Drapeaux & Étendards de la Révolution et de l'Empire*, Paris, Copernic, 1982.

Caulaincourt, General Armand de, *With Napoleon in Russia*, New York, William Morrow and Company, 1935.

Chevalier, Lieutenant Jean-Michel, *Souvenirs des guerres napléoniennes*, Editors Jean Mistler and Hélène Michaud, Paris, Hachette, 1970.

Chlapowski, Dezydery, *Memoirs of a Polish Lancer*, Chicago, The Emperor's Press, 1992.

Delderfield, R.E., *Imperial Sunset*, Philadelphia, Chilton Book Company, 1968.

Dupont, Marcel, *Cavaliers d'Epopée*, Paris, Lavauzelle, 1985.

– *Guides de Bonaparte et Chasseurs à cheval de la Garde*, Paris, *Les Editions Militaires Illustrées*, 1946.

Elting, Colonel John R., *Swords Around a Throne*, New York, The Free Press, 1988.

Fallou, Louis. *La Garde Impériale (1804–1815)*, Paris, *La Giberne*, 1901.

Grandin, F., *Souvenirs historiques du Capitaine Krettly*, Paris, Berlanselier, 1839.

Headley, Joel T., *The Imperial Guard of Napoleon*, New York, Charles Scribner, 1851.

Houssaye, Henry, *La Vielle Garde Impériale*, Tours, Alfred Mame, 1929.

JOB (Jacques Onfroy de Breville), illustrated by, *La Vielle Garde Impériale*, Tours, Maison Alfred Mame et Fils, 1902.

Johnson, David, *Napoleon's Cavalry and its Leaders*, London, B.T. Batsford, 1978.

Lachouque, Henry, *Napoléon et la Garde Impériale*, Paris, Bloud & Gay, 1956.

Manceron, Claude, *Austerlitz*, New York, W.W. Norton & Company, 1966.

Masson, Frédéric, *Cavaliers de Napoléon*, Paris, Boussod, Valadon et Compagnie, 1895.

Parquin, Denis Charles, *Napoleon's Army*, London, Longmans, Green, 1969. Reprinted Greenhill Books, 1987.

Picard, L., *Cavalerie de la Révolution et de l'Empire*, Saumur, *Librairie Militaire S. Milon Fils*, 1895.

Pigeard, Alain, *Les Étoiles de Napoléon. Maréchaux, Amiraux, Généraux 1792–1815*, Editions Quatuor, Entremont-le-Vieux, 1996.

Quennevat, Jean-Claude, *Atlas de la Grande Armée*, Paris-Bruxelles, Editions Sequoia, 1966.

Regnault, General Jean, *Les Aigles Impériales. 1804–1815*, Paris, Editions J. Peyronnet, 1967.

Rigondeau, Albert (RIGO), *Le Plumet, Planches 21, 22, 25, 26, 27, 36, 58*, Paris, RIGO Editeur.

Rogers, Colonel H.C.B., *Napoleon's Army*, New York, Hippocrene Books, 1974.

Rousselot, Lucien. *L'Armée Française. Ses Uniformes – Son Armement – Son Equipment.*
Planche No. 69. Chasseurs à cheval de la Garde. 1800–1815.
Planche No. 70. Chasseurs à cheval de la Garde. 1800–1815.
Planche No. 83. Chasseurs à cheval de la Garde. Trompettes. 1800–1815.
Planche No. 94. Chasseurs à cheval de la Garde. Officiers. 1800–1815.
Planche No. 23. Garde Impériale. Grenadiers à cheval. 1804–1815.
Planche No. 45. Grenadiers à cheval de la Garde. Trompettes. 1804–1815.
Planche No. 13. Garde Impériale. Dragons. 1806–1814.
Planche No. 53. Garde Impériale. Dragons. 1806–1814 (II).
Planche No. 47. Chevau-légers Polonais de la Garde. 1807–1814.
Planche No. 65. Chevau-légers Polonais de la Garde. Trompettes. 1807–1814.
Planche No. 75. Chevau-légers Polonais de la Garde. Officiers 1807–1814.

Sabretache, Carnet de la, No. 3, 1958; No. 6, 1961; No. 6, 1966; No. 5, 1969; No. 30, 1975; No. 53, 1980; No. 83, 1986; No. 109-E, 1991; No. 138, 1998.

Saint-Hilaire, Emile, *Histoire anecdotique, politique et militaire de la Garde Impériale*, Paris, Eugène Penaud et Compagnie, 1847.

– *Histoire de la Garde Impériale*, Paris, Eugène Penaud, 1847.

– *Histoire Populaire de la Garde Impériale*, Paris, Adolphe Delahays, 1854.

Thomason, Captain John W. Jr., *Adventures of General Marbot*, New York, Charles Scribner's Sons, 1935.

Tradition, Nos. 42–3, 47, 53, 59, 72, 73, 92, 103, 108, 124/125.

Tranie, J. & Carmigniani, J.C., *Les Polonais de Napoléon*, Paris, Copernic, 1982.

Wathier, R., *Les Timbaliers de la Grande Armée*, Paris, *Editions de la Sabretache*, 1980.

Willing, Paul, *Napoléon et ses Soldats. L'Apogée de la Gloire*, Arcueil, *Les Collections du Musée de l'Armée*, 1986.

– *Napoléon et ses Soldats de Wagram à Waterloo*, Arcueil, *Les Collections du Musée de l'Armée*, 1987.

Zaluski, General Comte Josef, *Les Chevau-légers Polonais de la Garde (1812–1814)*, Paris, *Librairie Historique F. Teissedre*, 1997.